# Also Called Sacajawea

| DATE DUE | RETURNED |
|---|---|
|  |  |
|  |  |
|  |  |
|  |  |
|  |  |
|  |  |
|  |  |
|  |  |
|  |  |
|  |  |
|  |  |
|  |  |
|  |  |
|  |  |
|  |  |

# Also Called Sacajawea

Chief Woman's Stolen Identity

Thomas H. Johnson
*University of Wisconsin–Stevens Point*

with
Helen S. Johnson

WAVELAND

PRESS, INC.

Long Grove, Illinois

For information about this book, contact:
Waveland Press, Inc.
4180 IL Route 83, Suite 101
Long Grove, IL  60047-9580
(847) 634-0081
info@waveland.com
www.waveland.com

Copyright © 2008 by Waveland Press, Inc.

10-digit ISBN 1-57766-534-1
13-digit ISBN 978-1-57766-534-2

Printed in the United States of America

7   6   5   4   3   2   1

*For the Eastern Shoshone people*
*Ah-ho.*
*Thank you.*

# Contents

# Acknowledgments

The real authors of this book are the Shoshone people who I knew during many years of fieldwork at Wind River. They provided the information that led to the discovery of the Wind River Sacajawea's true identity. I especially want to thank the family I remain closest to at Wind River, the Wesaws. By allowing me into their family life, they taught me valuable lessons. Tom Wesaw's children, especially Delmar, Tommy, and Marian, helped me over the years in many ways. Other descendants of Tom Wesaw's grandparents, John and Julia Enos, helped, especially Louis Enos and Felicia Kennah.

I thank the members of the Shoshone Business Council for allowing me to work on the reservation, with special thanks to council members Starr Weed and Gilbert Day for inviting me to meetings of the Native American Church, and to Bob Harris, longtime chair of the council for his dedication to the welfare of the Shoshone people.

The Bonatsie and Nipwater families of Big Wind River inspired me always; they are real fighters for causes involving the Shoshone. They seek to preserve Shoshone traditions and have never forgotten the importance of keeping their culture alive in spite of many pressures to conform to the white man's ways.

There are many individuals among the Shoshone who deserve special thanks. I can only single out a few. Maud and Harold Clairmont showed me much hospitality when I stayed at Vernon's Motel. Maud's uncle and aunt, Bud and Esther LeClair, allowed me to stay at their place and introduced me to a real Wyoming roundup.

Herman and Daisy St. Clair gave me encouragement and allowed me to enter the sacred Sun Dance, along with Tom Wesaw and his son George and Sun Dance leaders Johnny Trehero and Tissiwungo "Pine Tree" Gould.

Jack and Millie Guina, their families, the Roberts family, and others who live on Sage Creek, including Alfred and Audrey Ward, provided hospitality and made beautiful Shoshone beadwork for me that I cherish.

James Trosper gave me insight into Shoshone Sun Dance traditions, as did Irene Pingree and Benny LeBeau.

As a student, I spent much time learning the Shoshone language with Rupert Weeks, Tommy Wesaw, and Randy Tassitsie. Their helpfulness, patience, and generosity will always be remembered.

No anthropologist works in a vacuum. Demitri B. Shimkin did fieldwork among the Shoshone in the 1930s and, as my graduate advisor at the University of Illinois in the late 1960s, provided much of the background information to the Eastern Shoshone in a number of publications. By interviewing people like Polly Shoyo who lived as early as the 1840s, he laid the groundwork for the discovery of who Paraivo was. There are many other undiscovered heroes that time has forgotten but Paraivo has been rescued for posterity.

Sara Wiles, an anthropologist, and Steve Wiles, her spouse, kept me in touch with the people at Wind River while I was away and welcomed me and my family time after time as we made the long trek from Wisconsin to Wyoming. Sara's valuable work with the Northern Arapaho is also a fund of information. Thank you, Sara and Steve.

Thanks also to Wyoming historian Todd Guenther, a colleague and a resource. Many thanks to Alice Beck Kehoe for her belief in the importance of the restoration of Paraivo's rightful place in Shoshone history. We are especially indebted to editors Tom Curtin and Jeni Ogilvie for their encouragement and guidance.

The University of Wisconsin–Stevens Point made additional, culminating research on this project possible through a summer research grant and sabbatical.

The Shoshone people have become strong during the years I have known them, and this book is a tribute to their persistence in righting the wrongs that they and so many Native people have encountered. No book is without errors or omissions or misrepresentations. I take responsibility for any found here.

Some names and characteristics of living people have been changed to protect privacy.

Thomas H. Johnson
*Stevens Point, Wisconsin*

# Also Called Sacajawea

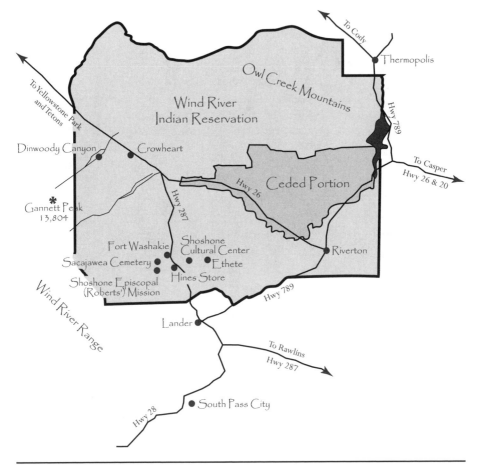

**Wind River Indian Reservation and Surrounding Area, Wyoming**

# Chapter 1

# Here Lies Sacajawea

I didn't go to the Wind River Indian reservation to improve conditions or to change people's lives. My job as an anthropologist was to listen to whatever the Eastern Shoshone wanted to tell me, to write it down, to faithfully report and not to impose my own views.

Before the reservation, the Eastern Shoshone lived in the Green River area of Southwestern Wyoming. The white trappers and traders used to call them the Green River Snakes because the sign for Shoshone is the curving hand motion through the air of a slithering snake. In those days, Shoshone bands, seminomadic groups of from 50 to several hundred, were known by the food they commonly ate—the Salmon Eaters, the Buffalo Eaters, the Sheep Eaters. There were many bands scattered throughout the Rockies and onto the Plains, from Saskatchewan to Texas and west to California.

Today the Yamp-Root Eaters are the Comanche. Until the early 1800s, they and the Shoshone were one people. The Eastern Shoshone remained in Wyoming, while the Comanche moved south to Colorado and Texas. There's a story that the final rift occurred in the late 1700s at Split Rock near Muddy Gap, Wyoming, because of a great epidemic, possibly the smallpox epidemic of 1782.

All the Shoshone were seminomadic, meaning they moved seasonally from sheltered areas in the winter to the Plains in the summer, following the food supply. But since about 1870, the Wind River reservation is home for the Eastern Shoshone. The reservation is in the western part of Wyoming where the Great Plains meet the Wind River range of the Rockies, most of it rangeland sloping away from the mountains. The mountains are the highest in Wyoming, almost 14,000 feet, and form the Continental Divide. Rivers—the Big Wind, the Little Wind, the Popo Agie—rush down the mountains through the canyons.

There's a thermal spring, too, but almost no recreational development. The Shoshone have resisted becoming another Jackson Hole. This is their place, reserved for them, and has been since well before the invasion of whites. Deep canyons cut the mountain range; some contain ancient carvings on the canyon walls and old burials, too. In recent years, chain-link fences have sprung up to guard against vandalism. Roads into canyons are closed.

The United States government's 1868 Treaty promised that the Eastern Shoshone would be the sole occupants of the Wind River reservation. But after the warfare between the Plains tribes and the United States had ended, the Northern Arapaho were homeless, and the United States found it convenient to deposit them at Wind River. No treaty placed the Northern Arapaho at Wind River but at Wind River the Northern Arapaho remain, as they have since 1878, simply by executive order.

An irrigation ditch separates the Arapaho settlements from those of the Eastern Shoshone who live to the west, mostly on small acreages or, more recently, in housing developments. The main Shoshone settlement is an old army post called Fort Washakie, after the famous Shoshone chief. Some old stone barracks and stables are still there and are now used for storing road equipment. The Wind River Indian Agency is in Fort Washakie, as well as the health clinic, tribal offices, a nursing home, and the main Shoshone community center, Rocky Mountain Hall. If you were to take all the official buildings out of Fort Washakie, there would be a small collection of white frame houses, mostly from the 1920s to the 1950s for employees. A post office and a gas station are pretty much the only businesses. For groceries, you drive a mile down the highway to the general store next to the trading post operated for tourists.

The reservation's land contains significant amounts of oil and natural gas. Profits from their sales provide a steady per capita income for the Shoshone and the Arapaho. The total income of the reservation is divided in half between the two tribes and a portion is allocated to each enrolled member of the Eastern Shoshone and Arapaho tribes. The Arapaho population is more than twice that of the Shoshone today, which means the income of each Arapaho is less than half that of each Shoshone. Even so, the Shoshone per capita income is usually less than $400 a month.

Employment opportunities are limited. There's ranching; there's fire fighting and working in the national forests; there's working for the tribe or the Bureau of Indian Affairs. The nearest town of any size is Lander, population 7,000, a few miles south of the reservation boundary or about 15 miles from Fort Washakie. Lander is mostly white and has little industry except the National Outdoors Leadership School, a recreational training program for well-to-do outsiders. In 2004, *Outdoors* magazine listed Lander as a "dream town." It's a dream for summer recreation or retirees with money from the outside world, perhaps, but Lander is primarily a service town for surrounding ranches and the several thousand Shoshone and Arapaho on the Wind River Indian reservation.

When I first came to Wind River in 1966, my hosts Maud and Harold Clairmont took me around the reservation. We drove past the cemetery named after Sacajawea, and the Clairmonts told me a little about her, that she'd come back to Wind River as an old woman and had died there. I had learned in school about the Indian teen who traveled with the Lewis and Clark expedition, of course: that Hidatsas had kidnapped her as a girl; that they had sold or traded or gambled her away to a French Canadian trader; that she gave birth to the trader's son; that as a member of the Lewis and Clark expedition of 1804–06 she had carried her papoose across half a continent; that she jumped into a river to rescue expedition items from a capsized pirogue; that she saw a beached whale on the Oregon coast. I hadn't even thought about what had happened to the young woman and her papoose after the expedition.

I went back on my own to visit the cemetery. My dad operated a monument business in Iowa, and I had worked summers setting monuments for him so I never had a fear of cemeteries. Besides, the inscriptions on tombstones are family records and family history interests me. It was early June, just a couple of weeks after Memorial Day. Artificial flowers decorated every grave. I remembered my dad saying that the quality of a community can be judged by how well it commemorates its deceased. A dry tangle of weeds grew in crazy profusion in the cemetery but the graves themselves were beautifully kept.

And then I walked to the log cabin at the crest of the hill. Reverend Davis, the current Episcopal missionary, had told me that it was one of the oldest buildings in the area. Originally a schoolhouse, it had been moved to the cemetery to serve as a mortuary chapel. Now it was falling down.

Standing by the old log chapel on that day in June, squinting against the sun at the backside of the monuments to Sacajawea and her family, I had no idea how many Shoshone I would later come to know and how many times I would return to visit them over the next 40 years. I hadn't yet heard their family stories or talked with spiritual and tribal leaders or danced in the Sun Dance. It wasn't until many, many years later that I realized how all these pieces fit together. Everything told the true story of the woman buried in the cemetery, the woman who also came to be called Sacajawea.

It took me years to listen deeply enough, years to understand who the woman in the grave really was.

# Chapter 2

# Mistaken Identity

Highway 287 leads through the Wind River Reservation and the foot-hills of the Wind River mountain range. Past the town of Lander, there are scattered ranches that give way to clusters of houses and trailers. Extended family members live near one another out here.

Welcome to Indian Country. Some of this land is divided into allot-ments belonging to the Eastern Shoshone and the Northern Arapaho peo-ples. It's been this way since the late 1800s when the government parceled out land to families and individuals as a result of the Dawes Severalty Act. The idea was to hasten the progress in getting Indians to live as whites, one homestead per nuclear family. The U.S. government wanted Indian people to live in self-supporting farms or ranches, and mandated that an economic unit should consist of the head of a family (usually a father) plus spouse and children, and that the family holding should consist of 160 acres of land, plus 40 additional acres for each minor child, with larger units for ranches consisting of grazing land only. This was considered a generous amount of land to support a family by U.S. standards at that time. How-ever, it did not account for the nature of the economic units in most Indian societies, which were based on communal hunting and gathering. Most Indian families also did not have the capital to run a farm or ranch, and many had lived in a traditional hunting and gathering way of life until that time. Additionally, most Indian societies were organized around kinship groups that were larger than the nuclear family and included many rela-tives on both sides. Elders of such groups were responsible for the social and economic well-being of a much larger kin group than our current American nuclear family of parents and their children. Most were not pre-pared socially or economically to benefit from the Dawes Act.

From the beginning of the reservation system, the United States gov-ernment not only determined the size of land to be set aside for Indians but also how it was to be used. Because they were a conquered people thought to be "primitive," the United States continued to control the use of reservation land after passage of the Dawes Act. Most of the land, therefore, does not truly belong to the Indians, in the way white America understands ownership. The United States government holds this land in trust. It is occupied and used or even leased—but not owned—by most of these families. Indians deemed educated and responsible (not "primitive") and able to support themselves in a cash economy could obtain a patent on land on reservations, and thus they could have custody of that land as long as they paid fees—or taxes. They could then control who inherited that land, which was taken out of trust status and controlled by Indians much as ordinary U. S. citizens.

It's always been hard for families to get enough money and land together to build a successful farming or ranching operation, even with irrigation. The land is good but out here only ten to twelve inches of rain fall each year.

A few miles into the reservation, Ray Lake glimmers and glints in the sun. It's a large reservoir for irrigation and was begun by Captain Patrick Henry Ray, an Indian agent in the 1890s. Indian agents, or superintendents, were appointed by the Bureau of Indian Affairs, which was run by the Department of the Interior, whose secretary was appointed by the President. While tribal councils could advise agents, agents had and still have enormous decision-making authority over reservations.

Ray was at Wind River when the United States government tried to implement a plan to create homesteads of 160 or more acres for each Indian family. Ray believed the allotment act was a ruse that encouraged Indians to lose their land. He was right, and because of his vocal criticism, along with his attempts to force white squatters and cattle barons off Indian land, Ray was run off the reservation by some local whites.

Past Ray Lake, there's an imposing new church building, the church of Jesus Christ of Latter Day Saints, a largely non-Indian congregation. The Shoshone-owned shop called Ancient Ways, sellers of Indian jewelry, beadwork, skins, hides, herbs, and beading supplies isn't far beyond. An acrid smell drifts from behind the metal building; the smell comes from the traditional tanning operation out back that uses brains to soften the hides.

A mile or so further up the road next to the Hines General Store is the Wind River Trading Post; both businesses are run by the non-Indian Hines family. The trading post is a long, low-slung building in the false-front tradition of the West. Most of what's for sale appeals only to tourists. So it's no coincidence that directly across the highway sits a granite boulder. Its bronze plaque reads:

# SACAJAWEA
## GUIDE OF THE
## LEWIS AND CLARK
## EXPEDITION
## 1805
## DEDICATED BY THE
## HISTORICAL LANDMARK COMMISSION OF WYOMING
## 1941

---

### GRAVE 2 MILES WEST

---

A July morning, the summer of 2006, I remember that signs pointing west to the grave used to exist. I ask at the trading post, "Aren't there any other signposts from the highway?"

The Shoshone woman at the cash register purses her lips and looks me over. She recognizes me vaguely, just as I recognize her vaguely. I buy gifts here every time I come out to Wyoming.

"It was the state of Wyoming that declared Sacajawea's grave to be a historical landmark. They are responsible for placing signposts to her grave, not the tribe," she says, without any attempt to hide her exasperation.

I wonder, is she asked the same question a thousand times or is she just annoyed by another example of the government not holding up an agreement? Probably both, I decide, and I take the map she holds out to me. I don't need it; I want the map just for curiosity's sake. We get to talking about a book for sale in the store. The book spells Sacajawea as a Hidatsa word with a *g* instead of a *j*—Sacagawea, meaning Bird Woman.[1]

A quick upward glance. "They got it wrong," the woman says. "Sacajawea was a Shoshone name. It means Boat Pusher." She turns to a tourist trying to pay her for a postcard. "Sacajawea came back as an old woman and died here," she tells the tourist. "I'm related to Sacajawea. So are a lot of us Shoshone."

The tourist is impressed.

Outside, I look at the map she'd given me. All the tourist spots are on it—the original Shoshone Agency, Reverend John Roberts' Mission, the Shoshone Tribal Cultural Center, the Chief Washakie Cemetery, and the Sacajawea Cemetery. With my index finger, I trace a right turn at the crossroads of the highway and Trout Creek Road. In my mind, I'm going to the tribe's Cultural Center. I like the place because it has a large display of historical photographs. One of those photographs is of me as a young man. It was taken outside the Sun Dance Lodge and I'm in full Sun Dance attire, all loaned to me by one of my Shoshone friends.

I get in my Jeep and decide to turn left up Trout Creek Road, to the west. It is very hot today. Cicadas sing in the hedgerows. The irrigated land along Trout Creek is green with alfalfa. I take a right, past Reverend Roberts' Shoshone Episcopal Mission and see a large wooden sign, weathered and worn, pointing right, up the hill toward the Sacajawea Cemetery. At least one sign is still in place. I turn and soon the words *Sacajawea Cemetery* in metal letters forming an arch over the entrance come into view. My Jeep bumps over a cattle guard and crunches over the limestone gravel in the parking lot at the foot of the cemetery.

It's just before noon and despite the heat and intense summer sun, I am not alone here this morning. There's a family of tourists on their way to Yellowstone and the Grand Tetons. Their van has a California license plate. They barely stop at the graves but move on to the top of the hill to look at the more impressive colored bronze statue of Sacajawea. They're standing by it now, pointing, clearly surprised to find a large statue out here.

I watch them pose for photos in front of her and then I myself start to walk. Here are family gravesites. There are Bonatsies, St. Clairs, Pingrees—all well-known Eastern Shoshone families. Some of the older graves are marked by iron bedsteads or white-painted stones with black painted lettering. In recent years, granite headstones have become more common. A foot-worn path with stepping stones leads past recent graves. I stop a moment here and there, remembering the easy laugh of one and the twist of slender hands of another when she talked.

Entrance gate to the Sacajawea Cemetery, Wind River Reservation, Wyoming.

The idea of a cemetery reserved for the burial of the dead is a Euro-American practice begun by the agents and missionary John Roberts at Wind River. Traditionally, the Shoshone placed remains of their dead in remote locations in the mountains far from settlements; remains were not visited, as their spirits stayed in those places. Spirits of the dead had unusual power; dwellings where someone had died were traditionally destroyed, and visiting graves or decorating them would have been unthinkable. Even today, Shoshone shun canyons known to have been burial areas. The influence of the missionary in changing these attitudes must have been strong, and many Shoshone must have silently objected to those changes. Those changes underscore the power the white authorities had in making the Shoshone conform to the dominant culture.

The sound of irrigation water from the ditch that bypasses the cemetery and a bird's high-pitched *tsee-tsee* drift on the breeze, hot as an oven. The cemetery earth is dry, dusty, weedy. The artificial flowers have been here since Memorial Day, stuck at the foot of graves, around tombstones, in vases. The breeze picks up and flutters the little American flags dotting the veterans' graves.

Fifty paces up the hill, the path arrives at three monuments in gray granite. The middle stone is the largest, maybe seven feet tall. It has an intentional rough-hewn surface, as if someone had chiseled it out of a mountain. The lettering is bold, deep, and carved to last. It's an expensive monument, erected in 1963 by the Wyoming State Organization of the National Society of the Daughters of the American Revolution.[2] The monument stands in honor of Sacajawea.

Some say there's no body in the grave, that family removed it and placed it in a secret location in the mountains. But this morning, a dream catcher with an eagle feather hangs from a top corner of the monument and moves with the breeze. Red earth is freshly-mounded up in front and newly-placed scalloped garden edging outlines the mound. Strewn over the red earth in front are blue beads, cowrie shells, an abalone shell and an abalone-shell button, rose quartz, polished agate, crystals, marbles, a rosary, a wooden crucifix, a silver angel, pennies, nickels, dimes, a plastic figure of an Indian in a war bonnet, a red-and-white resin snowman, eagle feathers, and an abundance of bright artificial flowers. There are so many offerings that the mound of red earth is barely visible. It's as if this were a new burial, not what it actually is: possibly the last resting place of a woman who died in 1884, said to be Sacajawea.

Her papoose Jean-Baptiste Charbonneau, grown to be an old man, and Bazil, said to be her adopted son, presumably lie on either side of her. But only Bazil is really buried there; he was moved from a traditional resting place in the mountains, even though it's very much con-

Grave offerings and decorations at the base of the Sacajawea monument. Erected in 1963 on the Wind River Reservation, Wyoming.

trary to Shoshone custom to disturb a body. Reburial is unthinkable to the traditional Shoshone. Any disturbance of a burial site risks bad luck for the living.

Baptiste's grave is empty. The actual remains lie deep in the canyons of the mountains behind the cemetery. You'd never know it by his headstone.

The three granite monuments stand in a row—Bazil, Sacajawea, Baptiste. An elaborately carved white bench has been provided. It is a good place from which to ponder the three monuments. More than seventy years ago, a white woman named Grace Hebard envisioned the bench here, just as it is today. She wanted people to contemplate Sacajawea, an American heroine who triumphed over great odds. As you sit on the bench, you are to turn to face the wide, shimmering expanse of Wyoming grassland to the east and imagine the Shoshone as they once were, the greatest horse nomads of the Plains.

Without Grace Hebard, there would be no Sacajawea Cemetery. She named the cemetery and paid for the headstones of Bazil and Baptiste herself and for a third tombstone, too—this one for a, as the tombstone reads, granddaughter of Sacajawea, Barbara Meyers. The stone is modest local gray granite, poorly engraved and placed behind that of Baptiste.

Before this became the Sacajawea Cemetery in about 1933, it was the Episcopal Mission Cemetery. Under President Grant's Peace Policy

Monument to Bazil next to the Sacajawea marker. Donated by Grace Hebard. Photo by Sara Wiles.

Monument to Baptiste Charbonneau who was misidentified as the son of Saca-jawea of the expedition. This is also next to the Sacajawea marker. Wind River Reservation, Wyoming. Photo by Sara Wiles.

in the early 1870s, missionaries were assigned to administer Indian reservations. James Patten, a lay minister, and Dr. James Irwin, both Episcopalian, were assigned to Wind River and served alternately as agents from 1870 to 1884. By 1883, a permanent Episcopal missionary, Welshman John Roberts, came to Wind River to convert the Shoshone. The mission was given land, and Roberts established a boarding school for Shoshone girls and baptized Chief Washakie and many Shoshone in the 1890s. From the 1880s to his own death in 1949, Reverend Roberts buried his converts here. In the center of his cemetery, Roberts' log chapel still stands, groaning, leaning, in need of restoration. Today most Shoshone still bury their dead here, even if they are not connected to the mission or baptized.

Usually, Christian cemeteries are named after a parish or a saint. There are cases where a cemetery is named after something secular, maybe a battle or a landmark. But this cemetery is different. The cemetery is named after the woman who accompanied Lewis and Clark. That woman never set foot in Wyoming. Long after her death, she was transformed into a heroine. Through a series of fabrications on the part of the white authority structure and a badly researched report to the Bureau of Indian Affairs, the real identity of the woman who is said to lie in the grave—or in the mountains—has been covered up to suit the needs of whites who wanted and still want to make her into Sacajawea.

The deception began with the 1904 centennial of the Lewis and Clark expedition in St. Louis, Missouri, to recognize a century of progress from the 1803 Louisiana Purchase that opened up a large portion of the continent to expansion of the new United States of America. Part of that exposition included recognition of the Corps of Discovery, authorized by Thomas Jefferson, and led by Lewis and Clark 1804-1806. The exhibit included a statue of Sacajawea by sculptor Bruno Louis Zimm, of New York. His model was Virginia Grant of Wind River and it was selection of this model that began Grace Hebard's idea of discovering what Sacajawea's fate had been.

This was the Progressive Era in American political history. Common working men and women asserted their rights to better standards of living. The story of the Lewis and Clark expedition and the Indian girl who carried a papoose across the wilderness spoke to people's optimism, to the promise of unlimited opportunities in the United States, and to the pioneer spirit and the belief in progress. But on the Wind River Indian reservation there was little evidence of material comfort. The earliest census of the Shoshone, taken in the 1870s, indicates a population of about 1,200. By 1900, this number dropped to around 850, despite a high birthrate. Disease, especially tuberculosis, semistarvation, and poor living conditions, took their toll.

The bad news didn't stop there. Just four years after the Great Treaty of 1868 that gave the Eastern Shoshone their reservation, the United States government forced the tribe to cede valuable land, including the gold mines of South Pass and the Lander Valley. After treaties with the United States were made between the government and Indian tribes, the United States often altered treaties to shrink the size of the reserved land base. Agents were sent out to the tribes, and agreements were made, often under coercion. The tribes often had little choice but to cede land that whites wanted, since they were a conquered people.

In 1878, a United States government executive order placed the Northern Arapaho, an unrelated tribe and traditional enemies of the Shoshone, on the same reservation where they remain to this day. In 1896 the Shoshone sold the great hot spring at Thermopolis for $60,000. By 1904, the centennial of the Lewis and Clark expedition, the Shoshone were being pushed to cede two-thirds of the remaining reservation to non-Indian homesteaders. Desperately poor, tribal leaders had little choice but to accede to the demands of the United States.

Enter Grace Hebard, suffragette, surveyor, librarian, and trustee of the University of Wyoming, later professor of political economy. The centennial of the Lewis and Clark expedition ignited her interest. She wondered what had happened to the young Shoshone woman and her papoose after the expedition. No historian had written about that. She might be the first to discover the story!

Grace Hebard corresponded with Reverend John Roberts. Hebard believed that the woman would be discovered at Wind River. Why this was is hard to say, except that Sacagawea was Shoshone. But she was not Eastern Shoshone. Sacagawea was a Lemhi or Northern Shoshone from near Salmon, Idaho.

So strong was Hebard's gut feeling about Sacajawea "returning" to the Wyoming branch of the Shoshone that she spent the next three decades trying to convince others that she was right. Hebard believed that the Shoshone woman's remarkable epic did not end with the Lewis and Clark expedition. Sacajawea, Hebard decided, had the courage and opportunity to escape a brutal, stupid, polygamous husband (as Hebard characterized Toussaint Charbonneau) and take her place as an old woman honored among her people.

Except, of course, the Wind River Shoshone were not Sacagawea's people. No matter. Grace Hebard wrote first an article and then a book stating that Sacajawea had come back to Wind River.

In 1955, conclusive evidence that Sacagawea did not die at Wind River as an old woman came to light. Captain Clark's cash book turned up in a collection purchased by the Newberry Library in Chicago. The cash book covers the years 1825–28, and on its back cover Clark wrote the names of all the members of the expedition and their current status. After *Se-car-ja-weau*, he simply wrote *"Dead."* After the name of Sacagawea's son, he wrote "in Wertenburgh, Gy," meaning that Jean-Baptiste Charbonneau was with Prince Paul in Wurttemberg, Germany.[3]

Despite this and much more evidence to the contrary, the Wind River theory lives on even today. Grace Hebard's 1932 book has recently been reprinted. The marker is still out on the highway to direct tourists to the grave. The Sacajawea Cemetery has a new statue. In 2006, the Daughters of the American Revolution donated a banner honoring Sacajawea to the Eastern Shoshone Cultural Center. Not only is Sacajawea's burial place at Wind River set in stone and cast in bronze but the theory that she came back to her people has become a living legend.

From the first time I set foot at Wind River, I heard stories filled with pride from Wind River Shoshone about their relative, Sacajawea. Historians and whites have tried repeatedly to discredit what some Shoshone ancestors said about the woman buried at Wind River. Those who claim descent from her or believe the story because their elders told it to them have every right to be angry. It is embarrassing to be told, not only by non-Indian authorities but also by Idaho Shoshone relatives, that the woman who was with the Lewis and Clark expedition was not from Wind River and is not buried at Wind River.

Sacajawea memorial erected in 1963 by the DAR with old chapel in the background. Wind River Reservation, Wyoming.

There is a way out of this dilemma, though. It's one that doesn't discredit any Shoshone or Shoshone oral traditions. It's a way that honors the Shoshone and provides the missing link to explain who the Wind River Sacajawea really was. Some might consider this to be an impossible task but the author of the Wind River theory was Grace Hebard, not the Shoshone people. Shoshone oral tradition tells that the woman at Wind River, called Sacajawea by some local whites, was really a far more important woman. Shoshone testimonies and oral traditions reveal that many Shoshone have known all along who she truly was.

# Chapter 3

# How One Family Became Another

Tom Wesaw was a widower in his 80s, and I was happy to drive him around, cook with him, take him to visit people who asked for doctoring—he was well known as a native healer. Tom invited me to live with him for the company and because I could also help around the house. I pumped water, bought groceries, and built fires for the sweat ceremonies that were conducted for healing the body and soul. He helped me, too, just by allowing me into his life. But Tom went way beyond that, even buying me a table and a lamp so I'd have a place to write my field notes. People on the reservation referred to us as "Two Toms."

One evening, a call came that his son's brother-in-law had died. There would be a wake at their house. Old Tom, his son Tommy, who lived nearby, and I went to the wake, and on the way home Tommy told me that the deceased's family was descended from Sacajawea. The family's name had originally been Charbonneau, he said with great pride. This would be because they were descended from Jean-Baptiste Charbonneau, the papoose of the Lewis and Clark expedition.

It was the first time I had heard somebody refer to Sacajawea as a close relative. Our drive led us past Pearl Meyer's place, and Tommy told me that her husband was also descended from Sacajawea.

I filed all this in the back of my mind. After all, I was at Wind River to learn from living people, not dead ones. What bothered me a little was the last name Charbonneau. There weren't any on the reservation. The name had never appeared on any Wind River Indian census, all the way back to the 1870s. There were other French surnames among the Shoshone, like LeClair, St. Clair, and Lajeunesse. Generally, if a white man or

17

man of mixed ancestry married into the tribe, his surname would be used by his descendants. Why weren't there Charbonneaus on the reservation then or now? I was being told that the woman and the baby with the Lewis and Clark expedition had descendants at Wind River. What had happened to the Charbonneau name?

A few years later, I came across some articles about the papoose of the expedition, Jean-Baptiste Charbonneau. A writer in Oregon named Irving Anderson had evidence that Jean-Baptiste had died near Danner, Oregon, in 1866.[1] That would mean the man buried as Jean-Baptiste Charbonneau in the Sacajawea Cemetery at Wind River couldn't have been the son of the young Shoshone woman who had accompanied the Lewis and Clark expedition. The man buried at Wind River didn't die until 1885 and it was at Wind River, not Oregon. If the Wind River man was not Jean-Baptiste Charbonneau, was there also a mistake about the woman buried as Sacajawea?

I began to dig in the archives to satisfy my curiosity and to understand how the Wind River Sacajawea took shape. It is a convoluted story based on one woman's hope of finding out what had happened to the young Shoshone woman after the expedition, a hope that refused to die.

In 1904, a professor at the University of Wyoming gave a talk about the Louisiana Purchase Exposition held in St. Louis that year.[2] A librarian named Grace Hebard was in the audience. She had already read Eva Emery Dye's *The Conquest*, a fictionalized account of the Louis and Clark expedition. In novelist Dye's imagination, Sacagawea became the expedition's guide and pilot, a heroine emotionally strong enough to endure a relationship that could never be called a marriage, physically strong enough to carry a child from North Dakota to the Pacific and back, and knowledgeable enough to interpret for Lewis and Clark and to obtain horses from her Shoshone people for the trip over the Continental Divide. Sacagawea's romanticized deeds placed her on par with the Indian princess Pocahontas and the French heroine Joan of Arc![3]

But, Grace Hebard realized, no one had found out what had happened to the young Shoshone heroine after the conclusion of the Lewis and Clark expedition. Previously, Hebard had written to the missionary at the Wind River reservation, which was a good 250 miles over rugged mountains from Laramie, the university's seat. Her letter had directed Reverend Roberts to help the New York sculptor Bruno Louis Zimm in his search for a Shoshone girl to model for a statue of Sacagawea. The statue was to be shown at the St. Louis exposition. Reverend John Roberts had been able to satisfy the sculptor's search, finding a young woman, said to be of the "pure Shoshone type."[4]

Now Grace Hebard wrote to Reverend Roberts once again. She asked him to inquire locally among the Shoshone. Did anyone remember a

Sacajawea, a woman born about 120 years before—a woman who had been with the Lewis and Clark expedition?

Something about all this sparked Reverend Roberts' memory. He vaguely recalled burying a very old Shoshone woman during his first year at Wind River, 1884. He knew her not as Sacajawea but only as *Bazil umbia*, "Bazil's mother." He had listed her under that name in the parish record. Bazil was a well-known sub-chief.

This gave me pause. Reverend Roberts had not even known that the Wind River Shoshone called the old woman Paraivo. That the white missionary had recorded Paraivo's name simply as Bazil's mother indicates her importance to the whites came from her relationship to Bazil. I checked the Shoshone Indian census of 1877. There was the name Bazil's mother again. Surely if she had been known as the woman with Lewis and Clark, both the Indian agent who conducted the census and the missionary would have been told. Surely this would have been reported to Washington, D.C.

I looked at many reports, letters, and documents from 1871–1907, roughly the first 30 years of the Wind River reservation. None mention the name Sacajawea or Sacagawea or a person said to have been with Lewis and Clark. You might think that if a woman as important to the whites had lived among the Eastern Shoshone and had many descendants, some mention would have been made of her in the reservation superintendents' yearly reports to the Commissioner of Indian Affairs in Washington, D.C. But none of the reports of any superintendents before 1907, the year Grace Hebard published the Wind River Sacajawea theory as a journal article, mention that Sacagawea or Sacajawea or the woman who had been with the Lewis and Clark expedition was living or had ever lived at Wind River.

Wouldn't the famous Shoshone chief Washakie, who died in 1900, have known that Paraivo/Bazil's mother was Sacagawea of the Lewis and Clark expedition? Wouldn't he have known that Paraivo/Bazil's mother had rendered an enormous service to the United States and was at Wind River? The only record we have that even mentions Washakie and Sacajawea in the same breath is a 1941 letter to Reverend Roberts from a retired special agent at Wind River named Harry Wadsworth. Wadsworth tells the story of the placing of the concrete pedestal at Sacajawea's grave at Wind River in the early 1900s. Wadsworth had talked many times with Chief Washakie as a young man. "In one of our talks of the old days among the Shoshone," Wadsworth writes, "he [Washakie] mentioned Sacajawea, calling her 'that old woman, Basil's mother.' "[5]

Washakie is not equating Sacajawea with Bazil's mother. Wadsworth is. There is no indication that Washakie knew about Bazil's mother's presumed role in the Lewis and Clark expedition any more than the agents at Wind River did. If he had, the astute old chief would surely have told others about it, including an impressionable young special agent like Harry Wadsworth.[6]

In truth, no one had come forward to talk about the woman with the Lewis and Clark expedition at Wind River until Grace Hebard began to inquire about her. That's exactly what one of the Eastern Shoshone elders, Judge Ute, said in 1924.[7]

I began to read through the reports of agents of the Wind River reservation to the Commissioner of Indian affairs, and in an 1876 report to Washington, D.C., Agent James Irwin referred to the Eastern Shoshone as being "far less numerous than they were during the days of Lewis and Clark."[8] Irwin's reference to the expedition shows that he understood its importance and that he knew it had passed through the northern part of Shoshone country. Perhaps Agent Irwin had read the expedition's well-known journals; they had been published in several editions since 1814. But even though James Irwin was the agent during the first years of the reservation and knew Bazil and his mother, Irwin's reports to the Commissioner of Indian Affairs never mentioned Sacagawea at Wind River or a connection between Sacagawea and the Eastern Shoshone. His successor, S.M. Martin, agent when Bazil's mother died in April of 1884, didn't say anything about Sacagawea, either.[9]

Wouldn't the agents have told Washington, D.C., that Sacagawea was at Wind River if it would enhance the importance of the Shoshone and their agency in the eyes of the government? Wouldn't the great negotiators, Washakie or Bazil, have asked for a pension and special favors for Sacagawea?

Reverend Roberts did ask around at Wind River, as Grace Hebard had requested. He found one other white man who remembered Bazil's mother. Years later, he came up with one more. But up until Grace Hebard stirred the ashes, they had not given Bazil's mother a second thought. And strangely enough, all the foremost authorities who knew Bazil's mother to be the woman with the Lewis and Clark expedition were not Shoshone but white.

Reverend Roberts found James Patten, who had come into the Indian service in 1871 in the very earliest days of the Wind River reservation as an Episcopal lay-teacher and preacher. Patten was a friend of Reverend Roberts and had also served for a year or so as acting superintendent at the Wind River Indian Agency. In 1879 Patten left the Indian Service and moved to nearby Lander where he operated a pharmacy and dabbled in real estate.

Most of what Patten had to say about Bazil's mother did not come from direct experience but from Baptiste's son Wit-to-gan. Wit-to-gan's father's mother had led the *a-va-je-mear* across Crow country to the sea and back, carrying her son, then an infant, on her back. A-va-je-mear, Patten explained, meant the first Washingtons, otherwise called white men.[10]

That is not an accurate translation. A-va-je-mear means only *those who went by long ago*. This could be any number of expeditions, presumably of non-Indians. What is clear is that it could not have been Lewis and Clark. Clark traveled through Crow country via the Yellowstone and Madison Rivers. Lewis followed the Missouri River to the north through Blackfeet country.

Who could the a-va-je-mear have been? The Astorians, members of an expedition seeking furs and led by Wilson Price Hunt in 1811, were probably the first white men to cross Crow country—northern Wyoming and southeastern Montana, considerably north of where many Eastern Shoshone lived at that time. They encountered Shoshone off and on during the course of the expedition. Those Shoshone were reported as friendly, generous, and helpful.[11] It seems likely that this expedition was the a-va-je-mear that Bazil's mother encountered.

As acting agent during the temporary leave of the regular agent from 1877 to 1879, James Patten had made no mention in his reports of Sacagawea. After Grace Hebard began her inquiries, Patten had no explanation for why he and others, Shoshone and white, knew that a great American heroine had lived and died at Wind River but said nothing until Grace Hebard asked him, except to say that a reading of *The Conquest*, Eva Emery Dye's novel about the Lewis and Clark expedition, reminded him of Wit-to-gan's story about his grandmother being with the a-va-je-mear. Bazil's mother, Patten declared, would never have claimed she "introduced the first white men into this country, unless this was a fact, for in the eyes of her people, this would be considered not a meritorious action but treachery."[12]

After all, the Shoshone woman with Lewis and Clark had participated in one of the major expeditions the U.S. had conducted, and she had unwittingly but very definitely helped the government extend dominance over the region. Patten was playing on the common knowledge that Indians didn't admire other Indians who were traitors. Might this be the reason neither the old woman nor any of the Shoshone ever spoke about Lewis and Clark?

In a word: no. To suggest an intentional cover-up of her true identity because she would be considered a traitor is to completely misunderstand Shoshone–U.S. relations since the signing of the 1868 treaty and Shoshone participation in wars against the Sioux. The Shoshone had firmly allied themselves with the United States even earlier, and Washakie was known as a friend of the white man in reports going back to the 1850s.[13]

James Patten had spent too much time around the Shoshone not to know all this. He had to explain his own silence in earlier years. Yet after

Grace Hebard began her inquiries in 1904, Patten was more than willing to say how it all came back to him. He now remembered the old woman saying she had crossed the mountains to the Pacific with Lewis and Clark! Patten may have been silent for decades but when Grace Hebard asked, Patten's memory suddenly came alive.

In truth, even before their official alliance with the United States government, the Eastern Shoshone were economically connected to white trappers at rendezvous in the Green River country. An early pioneer who lived around Fort Bridger in the 1860s said that all the men at Fort Bridger knew that Paraivo (Bazil's mother) had been "on an expedition with white men."[14] Just "white men"—not necessarily Lewis and Clark. It was common knowledge, not a secret.

In those days, the Shoshone were known as the Green River Snakes because they lived around Fort Bridger and the tributaries of the Green River.[15] Marriage with the trappers and traders helped to cement Shoshone–white relations. Jim Bridger is said to have married a daughter of Chief Washakie. Wyoming's first permanent white settler, Jack Robertson, married Marook, a Shoshone woman, and their daughter Lucille married Robert Hereford, a Virginian, and had a large family.[16] A daughter of Bazil married Shade Large, a Missourian. A number of other white men had Shoshone wives, and by the 1870s, they and their offspring were already listed with French or English names, along with those whose names were Shoshone.[17]

But again, the name Charbonneau is nowhere to be found in the Eastern Shoshone Indian censuses. In 1877, Bazil's mother's other son, Patseese, is listed as Bat-tez, probably an anglicized form of his Shoshone name. Could that be the French name Baptiste, as in Jean-Baptiste, as in the name of Sacajawea's papoose, Grace Hebard wondered. Although the name Patseese/Bateez/Bat-tez (to give all the spellings) might be coaxed into Baptiste (and it appears that Hebard was the first to call him Baptiste, meaning that Patseese was never called Baptiste during his lifetime nor is it common usage among French speakers to shorten the name Jean-Baptiste to Baptiste), Patseese himself was a terrible fit for Jean-Baptiste Charbonneau. First, Patseese was illiterate. And then there is the matter of Patseese's age at his death in 1885. If he had been the papoose of the expedition he should have been 80 years old, but Reverend Roberts said "he did not look this old."[18]

How old someone looks is subjective. Illiteracy is not subjective. In about 1813, Captain Clark himself had become Jean-Baptiste Charbonneau's guardian and had seen to the boy's education. Prince Paul of Wurttemberg took Jean-Baptiste to Germany with him for further studies. Jean-Baptiste, then a young adult, spent more than five years between 1823 and 1829 under the prince's guardianship, traveling extensively in

Europe and learning several languages. After his return to the United States the conduct of Sacagawea's son indicates he had been abroad. Jean-Baptiste Charbonneau showed himself to be a cultivated, urbane man who could speak and write several European languages.[19]

All the signatures we have from him indicate that he never signed his name *Baptiste* but rather *J. B. Charbonneau* or *Jean-Baptiste Charbonneau*, and his handwriting indicates a well-educated man of the early 19th century. His fluency in several languages was typical of many offspring of Indian-white unions at the time. Jean-Baptiste's education was far superior to most whites of the 19th century. Only his mixed ethnic background impeded his acceptance into the highest society of his time.

When Jean-Baptiste Charbonneau returned to America in 1829, he chose to lead a life of adventure, much as his father had, guiding expeditions in the Rockies and working for the American Fur Company, along with the mountain man and trader Jim Bridger in the 1830s. He attended some of the trapper rendezvous, summer trade expositions in which American goods—knives, guns, cloth, beads—were traded for beaver pelts, and encountered the Shoshone many times. He was in Idaho and Wyoming in the 1830s but there's no evidence that he connected with Shoshone relatives. In 1845, he served as a guide to the Mormon Battalion in the Mexican War, ending up in California.[20]

Later research has shown he was an alcalde in California before it was ceded by Mexico, clerked in a hotel in Auburn, and died near Danner, Oregon, in 1866 on his way to the gold fields in Montana.[21] The local newspaper ran a death notice, as did the newspaper in Auburn, California. His burial place was designated a National Historic Site in 1973.[22] A monument to his memory was rededicated in Danner in 2000, with representatives from the Lemhi Shoshone and Hidatsa in attendance.

Today, research has uncovered many of the details of Jean-Baptiste Charbonneau's life. There are eyewitness accounts that identify him as the former papoose of the Lewis and Clark expedition. At a trappers' rendezvous in 1834, the traveler William Marshall Anderson wrote in his journal that he had met Jean-Baptiste who had been "born of the squaw mentioned by Lewis and Clark on their journey."[23] Certainly, Jean-Baptiste was well aware of the role his mother and father had played in the expedition. His last documented meeting with his father took place in 1823 at the Curtis and Woods trading post in what is now Kansas City, Kansas.[24]

Documents show Jean-Baptiste Charbonneau was in Shoshone country with Sir William Drummond Stewart in 1843 and was joined by a son and nephew of Captain Clark. Later that same year, he was in St. Louis to settle his father's affairs.[25] In fact, there's no record of Sacagawea anywhere after her death in 1812. Neither the son nor the nephew of Clark say anything about Jean-Baptiste visiting his mother or talking about visiting her while he was in Shoshone country. This would indicate that he had no reason to seek her out among the Shoshone.

To his credit, Reverend John Roberts, the first person to make the possible connection between Bazil's mother and Sacagawea, never could reconcile the image of the European-educated, highly literate, and well-traveled Jean-Baptiste Charbonneau with the illiterate Patseese of Wind River.

But Grace Hebard wasn't ready to give up. She decided that there was an explanation: the many years Jean-Baptiste had spent as a guide and trapper in the West had caused him to shed or forget his education. She wrote to a friend,

> It has been my observation that when Indians have been sent to Carlisle [a military school established in Pennsylvania for educating young Indian men], that reversion when they returned to their original environment happened often and they are not as satisfactory, desirable nor upright as they were before they came into contact with white men.[26]

To a colleague, she explained,

> I think there is absolutely no denying that Baptiste, Sacajawea's son, was abroad for six or seven years. Exactly how much knowledge he absorbed and retained is, to my mind, quite another subject. The Indian who has gone to Carlisle and graduated and has come back on the reservation, as the one of the Shoshones where Sacajawea lived, reverted. The call of the wild is too much for them and they spurn the knowledge which they have learned for fear that they might have to put it to actual use in some grinding occupation and they fly to the mountains to hunt and to the meadows to whip up and down the stream.[27]

In her eventual book about the Wind River Sacajawea, Hebard summed up what she thought had happened to Jean-Baptiste Charbonneau: "Baptiste in later life suffered the usual fate of the half-breed who deteriorates from adopting the vices of the whites."[28]

Prejudice of the time regarded someone like Jean-Baptiste Charbonneau as a "mule," reflecting the worst traits of two races. William Marshall Anderson, the traveler who met Jean-Baptiste at a mountain man rendezvous, would have disagreed. He described Jean-Baptiste as "an intelligent and interesting young man. He converses fluently and well in English, reading and writing and speaking with ease French and German—understanding several of the Indian dialects."[29] There is plenty of evidence from his years in California, too, that Jean-Baptiste Charbonneau was exactly what you would expect from his background.

In her last years, Paraivo lived with a man everybody said was her son (and she, his mother—hence the name *Bazil's mother* in the census and parish registry). Bazil—Shoshone name, Pa:si—was the more notable brother at Wind River. His name appears many times in reports written by United States agents and others in the Green River area of Wyoming. Bazil/Pa:si was an important man, a Sun Dance leader and one of the signers of both the 1863 Peace Treaty and the Great Treaty of 1868, and one of Washakie's sub-chiefs.

If Paraivo was really the woman who had traveled with the Lewis and Clark expedition, she couldn't have two natural sons, Grace Hebard reasoned, because the woman with the Lewis and Clark expedition was known to have given birth to only one boy. Pa:si/Bazil, she declared, must have been the son of Sacajawea's dead sister. A less respectable source served Grace Hebard's cause, the earlier Biddle Edition of the expedition journals. The Biddle Edition said that the young woman adopted the son of her dead sister when she was among her people, the Lemhi, in 1805.[30] The later, more authoritative editions of the expedition's journals, such as that of R. G. Thwaites (1904), make no mention of an adoption. Grace Hebard had access to them but decided she needed the adoption, so preferred the Biddle Edition.

Another bad fit. Reverend Roberts wrote *Bazil's mother* in his registry, not Bazil's aunt or adopted mother or stepmother. Pa:si (Bazil) and Paraivo lived in the same house at Wind River in the earliest days of the reservation. Patseese (Baptiste) arrived at Wind River three years later.[31] Why would Paraivo live with her adopted son and not her natural son? And why would the children of Maggie Large, a daughter of Pa:si, say that Paraivo "always called Bazil her son"?[32] It is true that the Shoshone language and kinship terminology use the word *bia* for mother and maternal aunt and those first cousins call each other brother and sister, not cousin. An adopted child could certainly call his aunt *mother* and she would call him *son*. But Hebard's work showed no awareness of Shoshone kinship terminology.

All the reports of Pa:si are from Wyoming, not Lemhi Country. If Pa:si were the adopted nephew, wouldn't he have originally come from the Lemhi in Idaho? To shore up this connection, Grace Hebard pulled out a man named Bazeel, mentioned in the journals of the Mormon mission to the Lemhi in 1856.[33] *Bazeel. Bazil.* Close enough for Grace Hebard. They must have been the same person, she said.

But Pa:si/Bazil was clearly in Wyoming in 1856, not Idaho, and is mentioned in the Utah superintendents' reports to the Bureau of Indian Affairs as being with Chief Washakie (Wyoming was then part of the Utah superintendency). He couldn't have been at the Mormon mission to the Lemhi at the same time. It took a long time to travel from northern

Idaho to southwestern Wyoming. "Chief Bazil seems to have been a popular after-dinner speaker," Grace Hebard threw out, almost laughing herself at the absurdity of the same person being in two widely separated
places at the same time, "for the three speeches here recorded occurred at
three different places—at Fort Supply and Fort Bridger (in Wyoming) and
at Fort Lemhi in Idaho."[34]

None of this explains why Pa:si was Paraivo's primary caretaker in
her old age, rather than Patseese who was supposed to be her only natural
son. It doesn't explain the difference in ability between Pa:si and his
brother, who was supposed to be Jean-Baptiste Charbonneau.

It's not surprising that I never heard the Charbonneau surname at
Wind River. It never existed there.

# Chapter 4

# Reservation and Town

Standing on the sidewalk in Lander on the Fourth of July, 1966, I watch the parade. Every service club, every church, every group of any size has a float. Between and around the floats are marching bands, mounted horse groups, and notables riding in convertibles, all waving that parade wave. The Shoshone have a float with a forest setting and a tipi. June McAdams is Sacajawea today. She's beautiful and she traces her descent five generations back to Sacajawea. June is sitting in front of the float's tipi, smiling, waving from the wrist with her fingers together.

Another Fourth of July in Lander almost four decades later, a granddaughter of Reverend John Roberts rides in the parade. The emcee tells us about her family connection with the pioneer missionary. Reverend Roberts has been dead more than fifty years but the emcee does not explain who he was. There is no need. Much of the crowd already knows.

But not all. There's been quite a turnover in the population of Lander in the last few years. In the 1990s, a national magazine rated Lander as one of the ten best places to retire. The location is attractive, close to the mountains where wind velocities are unusually low. There isn't any dirty industry like oil or coal in town. Real estate values are still relatively low because Lander doesn't have the cachet of Jackson Hole.

Lander does have the headquarters of the National Outdoor Leadership School or NOLS, founded about 30 years ago by Paul Petzoldt, a career outdoor enthusiast and mountain climber. The school has grown. It now owns the old Noble Hotel, built in the 1920s. The hotel once had a restaurant and a lobby full of furniture designed and made by Thomas Molesworth, in cowboy high-style with Navajo-inspired upholstery and inlaid Indian designs. The furniture was sold—rumor has it to former Disney CEO Michael Eisner—and now the hotel is a dormitory for the well-heeled wilderness enthusiasts who flock to Lander each summer.

The reservation is not open to outdoors enthusiasts; it's not a public recreation area, even if the part of the mountainous region owned by Indians cuts a large swath out of national forest territory that might otherwise be used for recreation. A NOLS outfitter informed me, "We tell our people they *must* stay off the reservation."

It isn't exactly that the Shoshone don't want tourism in the area. Sacajawea's grave is a tourist site, after all. The Shoshone have decided to build a casino between Fort Washakie and Lander that will bring many visitors to the reservation.

The town of Lander tries to attract tourism. Every summer, it welcomes the International Climbers Festival and hosts the Lander Brew Festival and a half-marathon. Most famously, Lander is the home of the One Shot Antelope Hunt. Held in the fall of each year, the One Shot welcomes celebrities from the worlds of entertainment, big business, and government. The Shoshone make them blood brothers to underscore the traditional ties of friendship between the Shoshone and important whites, ties that go back to the cordial relations between Chief Washakie and the trader Jim Bridger, the U.S. government, and the pioneer families of Lander—ties that go back to Ohamagwaya who preceded Washakie as chief.

But the Shoshone want to keep outsiders in their place. They don't want the reservation overrun with tourists wandering around with backpacks. They want outsiders to visit the historic sites and shop for souvenirs and otherwise leave them alone. It is not surprising that the Shoshone today see the reservation as a refuge from crass commercialism, aggressive land developers, hikers and backpackers and mountain climbers, and people in ATVs, SUVs, and pickup trucks. During the 1970s, as activists came to dominate the Shoshone and Arapaho business councils, no white person was allowed to set foot on the reservation, with a few exceptions. Recently, the only road to Dickinson Park, a popular camping area and trailhead just off reservation land in the mountains, was closed by individual Shoshone who own land over which the access road passes.

The Shoshone have come to accept the Arapaho presence on their reservation. On a political level, they live in an uneasy truce with them. Ever since the Arapaho arrived at Wind River, the Shoshone have believed that the United States government cheated them. By the early 1900s, it became clear that the government had no intention of moving the Arapaho to their own reservation. The Shoshone asked the Wyoming congressional delegation to pass an act to enable the tribe to sue the United States government for placing the Arapaho at Wind River. The act was passed by Congress in 1913.

This was a major victory for the Shoshone. Although they didn't expect the Arapaho to leave, they did hope to get some monetary compensation. The Shoshones' lawyer, George Tunison of Omaha, worked hard to get the claim acted on by Congress, but it was not passed until 1938 and the money was finally distributed the following year, 26 years after the enabling act. Even then, the compensation of more than $4,000,000 included the clause that, in the future, the assets of the reservation would be equally divided between the two tribes. The Shoshone had gained a partial victory but a very costly one.

Out of the $4,000,000, only $1.5 million was actually distributed to the Shoshone, and $2.5 million was withheld by the government in a special account. Even portions of per capita incomes from the Shoshones' own resources like oil and gas were withheld by the government for many years. The government simply did not trust the Indians' ability to handle so much money.

The rights of the invading whites have always taken precedence at Wind River. They had the power to lobby for a reduction of the size of the reservation in 1872, 1896, and 1904 and the power to withhold promises, especially if the Shoshone openly disagreed with exploitation. In 1907 just before he was to go to Washington, D.C., to complain that the Shoshone had not gotten the $150 promised to each of them for ceding lands, George Terry, chairman of the Shoshone Tribal Council, was brutally murdered in a mock "Indian" style tomahawk slaying that remains unsolved.

Not all whites have been enemies, however. A number of Landerites live on the reservation or work there, and some have married Shoshone. This goes back to the earliest contact between whites and Indians. The Lander radio station KOVE has a 10-minute program every weekday morning at 7:45 called Reservation News, but the Lander newspaper hardly covers the reservation. For that, you have to buy a copy of the weekly *Wind River News*. You see Indians occasionally on the streets of Lander or in the grocery stores but almost never in the restaurants and boutiques.

Dance performances in the summer are about the only Indian visibility in Lander these days. Several Landerites have told me that the local museum, now called the Museum of the American West, is run by a county board whose members don't want the Indians to be considered part of the county's history. The board has denied funds to the museum, leading to the resignation of its director, a professional historian.

Anti-Indian sentiment like this is nothing new but until recently was more muted. Just as there were always people in Lander with ties to the reservation who took the side of the Shoshone, there were Shoshone who played an important role in relations with whites in Lander. Herman St. Clair was such a man. The St. Clairs were descended from Chief Washakie's interpreter Narkok and related as in-laws to Pa:si. Herman's paternal grandfather was a white man and Herman's mother also had white ancestry, although Herman and his siblings were raised as Shoshone on the reservation. His brother Lynn had been one of Reverend John Roberts' catechists and had played the role of Roberts in a Sacajawea pageant in 1935. Sometimes Herman posed for photographs in a traditional ceremonial headdress and beaded buckskin. You can see his headdress on display at the trading post at Wind River. There is no chief of the Shoshone anymore, but in Herman's day the general public tended to think of him as representing the tribe.

When I first came to the area, Shoshone men in western hats and boots and older women in beautiful shawls and beadwork were often in the stores in Lander. The Nu Way Café was the place to have lunch, whether you were white, Shoshone, Arapaho, or even a bit of each. When I went to town with Tom Wesaw, everybody recognized him because of his distinctive low-crowned black western hat. Everyone knew everyone else and they all joked around and greeted each other. Tom's cousin Joe Kennah operated a men's clothing store called Joe's Place.[1] He always stocked those low-crowned black western hats especially for Tom. The Shoshone looked on Lander as their town, too. It was a place where merchants treated them decently and did not generally discriminate against them.

The business the Indians gave the town must have been a large percentage of the total trade, considering that the reservation population was greater than Lander itself. In those days, there were several men's and women's clothing stores, a couple of jewelry stores, at least three drug stores with soda fountains, several banks and insurance companies, a couple of hardware stores, a shoe store, four bars, and two hotels. Today, one of the jewelry stores still stocks turquoise jewelry from the Southwest but its array of local beadwork is gone. Most of the old-time businesses are gone. They either yielded to a couple of big box stores on the edge of Lander or became pricey boutiques, bookstores, restaurants, and coffeehouses for the newly arrived retirees and NOLS visitors.

Ever since the gold strikes in South Pass, a natural crossing point through the Rocky Mountains at the southeastern end of the Wind River Mountains, in the 1860s, newcomers have flocked to Shoshone country. The Shoshone remember the late 1800s when large cattle barons invaded their land and grazed animals for nothing. They remember that the beautiful reservation Washakie and his sub-chiefs were able to obtain was whittled down to a fraction of its original size. They remember that the Brunot Treaty of 1872 took valuable land from South Pass to the Lander Valley, which encompassed about one-third of the reservation, and included the fertile Lander Valley, site of the town of Lander. This enormous piece of real estate was given to the United States for a mere $25,000 to be divided into yearly payments of $5,000 for five years for the purchase of cattle to build up a herd for the Shoshone. They remember how half of the assets of the remaining reservation went to the Arapahos, all because the United States reneged on so many promises.

The theory that a great American heroine had returned to her people, had lived and died at Wind River, and had descendants there couldn't have come at a more favorable time. In 1904 two-thirds of the remaining reservation was ceded through the McLaughlin agreement to provide land to homesteaders. By this time, the Shoshone population had reached a new low; tuberculosis and other infectious diseases were rampant. The government annuities had run out. Necessities of life were dear and cash was scarce. As soon as they were allowed to sell their allotments, many Shoshone did just that. They used the money to buy enough food to eat; it was that simple.

Times were hard. The Sun Dance was banned during part of the early 1900s. Many Shoshone held the empowering Ghost Dance in secret because of the fear that it would be the next ceremony to be banned.

A new religion was sweeping through the Plains tribes. This was the Native American Church, a religious organization found among many tribes that included healing rituals involving the use of a cactus, peyote. It offered cures for illnesses, forbade alcohol, and stressed closer ties with other Indian nations. The story at Wind River goes that Charley Washakie, a son of the old chief, obtained the knowledge of the church from the Comanche in Oklahoma and introduced it to the Shoshone around 1900.

A few fortunate Shoshone had government jobs, whether they worked at the mill or dug irrigation ditches or worked for the Bureau of Indian Affairs. Most Shoshone eked out a living on their small allotments, raising vegetables, pasturing a few cattle, and hunting and fishing. Mostly, the Shoshone were at the mercy of the government and its agents, the white power structure. Paraivo, a group of whites said, was the woman who had accompanied Lewis and Clark to the Pacific and back, carrying an infant son on her back. How could the Shoshone say no?

Some doubted it, knowing their elders had never said anything about Paraivo being also known as Sacajawea until Grace Hebard, Reverend Roberts, and James Patten had told them about her.

Jennie Hereford Martinez, interviewed at the age of 92 in 1954, agreed.[2] Paraivo had been her closest neighbor in Bridger Country, before the reservation, even. Mrs. Martinez's testimony predates any of the recollections of Reverend Roberts, James Patten, or Dr. Irwin. It is based on years of knowing and interacting with Paraivo, Indian girl to Indian woman. In contrast, Reverend Roberts knew Paraivo so casually during the first year of his tenure at Wind River that he knew her only as Bazil's mother when she died. After all, he had only been on the reservation a year. Mrs. Martinez is a more reliable source of information than Reverend Roberts, James Patten, or Finn Burnett, an old pioneer. Paraivo visited Mrs. Martinez's mother daily. At no time did Mrs. Martinez hear Paraivo mention Sacajawea or Lewis and Clark.[3] To allege that Paraivo said nothing because of shame or fear is to dishonor Paraivo, her accomplishments, and her enormous prestige among the Shoshone.

How much sense does it make to say that Paraivo kept her identity secret but at the same time occasionally wore her Jefferson medal from the Lewis and Clark expedition in public?

# Chapter 5

# The Search for Proof
# You Can See and Touch

Grace Hebard seldom left the state of Wyoming or even her home base of Laramie. Originally from Iowa, she was born there to a minister and his wife in 1861. Hebard received her bachelor's degree in civil engineering from the University of Iowa in 1882 and obtained a Master's degree from Iowa in 1885 before the graduate college was organized. She could never say exactly what the degree was in.[1] Her 1893 Ph.D. from Illinois Wesleyan, a small Methodist institution, was in political economy, an academic discipline that studies the relationships between the political and the economic systems of a society, but she did her coursework entirely by correspondence and only had to appear on campus to take a final exam.[2] Years later, when she was asked, she couldn't remember the title of her research leading to the doctorate or even the general subject or even if she had done research leading to a doctoral dissertation.[3] Today, this kind of degree would never be honored.

Grace Hebard was an academic lightweight. In an era when advanced degrees were uncommon, hers could impress some people. A few years later, she passed the Wyoming State bar but never practiced law.[4] In 1894, she became librarian at the University of Wyoming, a position she held until 1919[5]. She was also a trustee of the university. The University of Wyoming had only just been formed in 1891. Grace Hebard got in on the ground floor of the institution.

Following the publication of her 1904 book on the history and government of Wyoming, Hebard was made an associate professor. Two years later, she received a promotion to head the Department of Political Economy, a position she held until her death in 1936.[6] At that time, land grant universities were required to offer a political economy course.[7] Somebody had to teach it, even if no one wanted to take it. At times, Hebard taught classes of only two or three students.

Hebard's theory of what had happened to Sacajawea made people sit up and take notice. Newspapers published articles about her startling find. It was big news. For a little over a decade after its first publication in 1907 as an article in the first volume of *The Journal of American History*, Grace Hebard's Wind River theory had no challengers.[8] It was the only answer to what had happened to Sacagawea. But in 1920 the publication of the journal of the clerk at Fort Manuel Lisa in South Dakota, 1812-1813, dropped a bombshell on the theory.[9] In his entry for December 20, 1812, John Luttig wrote that "this Evening the Wife of Charbonneau a Snake Squaw, died of a putrid fever she was a good and the best Woman in the fort, aged abt. 25 years she left a fine infant girl."[10]

The woman who died on December 20, 1812, had to have been Sacagawea. Here's why: Luttig calls her "the" wife of Charbonneau, so the deceased must have been the only wife of Charbonneau at the fort, even though he is reported to have had at least one other wife. An eyewitness report puts Sacagawea on a boat traveling up the Missouri in the spring of 1811. Henry Brackenridge, a lawyer fluent in French and therefore able to easily speak with Toussaint Charbonneau, reported that "we have and on board a Frenchman named Charbonet, with his wife, an Indian woman of the Snake nation, both of whom accompanied Lewis and Clark to the Pacific, and were of great service."[11]

The only person who was both an Indian woman of the Snake nation and a member of the Lewis and Clark expedition was Sacagawea. There are no travelers' accounts of her coming down the river after that. There are no reports from St. Louis that she returned after going up the river. This means that Sacagawea went up the river and stayed there. She undoubtedly stayed at the Mandan villages where she and Charbonneau were well-known. Charbonneau came back to St. Louis in the fall of 1811 but returned with Manuel Lisa and Luttig in 1812 to construct Fort Manuel Lisa, completed by October of that year.[12] Charbonneau was off again, but Sacagawea apparently moved into the new fort. A daughter, Lizette, had been born by that time, but on December 20, 1812, the "Snake Squaw" of Charbonneau died. After the fort was abandoned due to depredations of the Sioux, Luttig brought baby Lizette to St. Louis in 1813.

Grace Hebard cites Brackenridge's account of the trip up the Missouri with Charbonneau and Sacagawea in her 1907 article. She then did an unforgivable thing: she quoted Brackenridge's account in full and then simply denied its truth, saying that although Luttig says "Charbonet" came up the river with his Snake wife, both of whom had "accompanied Lewis and Clark," he lied.[13]

But Brackenridge would have had no reason to lie. It was Hebard who lied. She concocted a new story: the woman who later died at the fort was the "other wife" of Charbonneau, Otter Woman.[14] Later, she took her lie a step farther. She assumed—without any evidence—that Sacagawea remained in St. Louis with her son Jean-Baptiste instead of going up the river with Toussaint Charbonneau.

There is yet another reason the woman who died at Fort Manuel Lisa in 1812 had to have been Sacagawea. On the Lewis and Clark expedition's return trip down the Missouri in 1806, after leaving the Mandan villages, Captain Clark wrote to Toussaint Charbonneau promising to educate little Jean-Baptiste, if he and Sacagawea would bring the boy to St. Louis.[15]

This they did in 1809, coming back down river and having the boy baptized late that same year.[16] But even though Charbonneau acquired some land in Missouri (a bonus gift to members of the Lewis and Clark expedition), he apparently had no desire to farm it so he sold it to Clark for $100 in 1810. As Brackenridge reported the next year in his journal, Charbonneau and his "Snake wife" wanted to return to their previous life among the Mandan and Hidatsa of the Upper Missouri. As young as Jean-Baptiste was and as difficult as it must have been to leave a six year-old with a friend, Sacagawea and Toussaint Charbonneau had every reason to entrust the boy to Clark. After all, he had promised to educate the child he referred to as the "little dancing boy" of the expedition, the one he affectionately called Pomp, and he intended to keep his promise.[17]

After the publication of Luttig's journal in 1920 raised serious doubts about Sacagawea living beyond 1812, Grace Hebard had two choices: admit that the Wind River theory was wrong or continue to trace the woman's existence beyond the grave. She chose the latter and spent the next decade trying to prove the impossible. As a result, Hebard's Sacajawea became a fictional character, different from the historical Sacagawea. Sacajawea was "rediscovered" in the guise of another woman, Paraivo/Bazil's mother, and among a different group of Shoshone, those at Wind River.

Nothing better illustrates Hebard's capacity for the invention of history than how she used Charbonneau's second Shoshone wife in order to keep Sacajawea from coming up the river. Clark's journal tells us that Charbonneau did actually have a second Shoshone wife and that she remained behind during the expedition. The journals of Lewis and Clark do not give the second wife's name, nor do any accounts from the period. But a white man, James Schultz, a 20th-century author of historical fiction, gave her a name: Otter Woman. Schultz wrote about Otter Woman in 1918, a full 113 years after the Lewis and Clark expedition left the second Shoshone wife at the Mandan villages. Schultz claimed he had heard

about Otter Woman as a young man in Montana in the 1880s. Two eld-
erly Hidatsa had given him their account of Sacagawea's life, said to come
from Sacagawea herself.[18] The story goes that Otter Woman had been
Sacagawea's bosom companion and "she died shortly after the return of
the expedition" to the Mandan villages in 1806.[19]

Grace Hebard needed Otter Woman alive, not dead. And so she
totally discredited Schultz's account as "pure fiction" in her bibliographi-
cal reference to his book but used the name Otter Woman, conveniently
discarding her date of death.[20] Once again, Hebard took what bolstered
her Wind River Sacajawea theory and eliminated what would have discredited it. In order for Sacajawea to remain alive, another wife of Charbonneau had to die at Fort Manuel Lisa in 1812. So Hebard had Otter
Woman survive past her reported death in 1806 (even if fictional) so she,
instead of Sacajawea, could die in 1812.

Hebard used Otter Woman in another way. She made her the mother
of another fictional character, Jean-Baptiste's older half-brother Toussaint.[21] First, Hebard had to prove there indeed had been a Charbonneau
son by Otter Woman—all to keep Sacajawea alive and somewhere other
than Fort Manuel Lisa in 1812.

Here's what documents that are contemporary to the period tell us
really happened: after the death of Sacagawea on December 20, 1812,
John Luttig, clerk at Fort Manuel Lisa, took care of her infant daughter,
Lizette. Jean-Baptiste had remained in St. Louis where he was going to
school. We know this because the boy was not on the boat up the river
with Brackenridge and because Clark had promised to educate him. When
Fort Manuel Lisa was abandoned early in 1813, Luttig brought little Lizette to St. Louis. Their father, Toussaint Charbonneau, was erroneously
presumed to be dead, not having returned from a fur-trading expedition.
He did eventually come back to St. Louis by 1816 and lived until at least
the early 1840s but never assumed much responsibility for his children.[22]

In an orphan's court on August 11, 1813, John Luttig was named
guardian of the two Charbonneau children. The legal papers called the
son *Tousant* (sic) *Charbonneau*, and described him as about ten years old.
(Jean-Baptiste would have been eight.) There is no record of what happened to Lizette after this—she may have died. The guardianship proceedings are the last record we have of her existence.[23]

Eventually Clark, who had taken his family to Virginia for safety during the War of 1812, returned to St. Louis. Luttig died in 1815, and the
name of Clark—who was certainly the intended guardian—was inserted
in the court record.[24] No mention is made of Sacagawea in the legal documents, but because the documents name the orphans as Lizette and
Toussaint, not Jean-Baptiste, this was Hebard's opportunity to claim that
Otter Woman had been their mother.

Why would Clark have adopted the children of Otter Woman? Why would he have become the legal guardian of children he had never met before, the offspring of a woman he didn't know? The clear answer is that there never were two boys. There was only Jean-Baptiste, who was also known as Toussaint, much as we would call a boy "Junior." Clark himself referred to the boy by that name in his list of expedition participants in his cashbook years later when Jean-Baptiste was in Germany with Prince Paul.[25] This is the same cashbook that noted the word *dead* after Sacagawea's name in a list of expedition participants, all written in Clark's hand.

To shore up the claim of two sons of Charbonneau by different wives, Hebard misinterpreted the school and boarding expenditures that Captain Clark made for Jean-Baptiste in 1820.[26] On January 20, tuition for two quarters was paid to J. E. Welch for "J. B. Charboneau" (sic), a half-Indian boy. On March 31 payment was made to L. T. Honoré for board and lodging, again for J. B. Charboneau.[27] Payments were made again to L. T. Honoré for "J. B. Charboneau" in June and October, 1820. At the end of what would have been the school year, one payment for one quarter's tuition went to Father Neil for Toussaint. For Hebard, that one payment proved there were two different boys.

But there is a more likely interpretation of these records. Of the five payments for tuition and board and lodging listed, all are for J. B. Charbonneau, and the one payment listed for Toussaint is simply payment for the last month of the school term for J. B. Charbonneau, who was also known by Clark and others as Toussaint, after his father. Otherwise, Jean-Baptiste Charbonneau's tuition would have remained unpaid.

None of this negates the possibility that Toussaint Charbonneau Sr. might have sired other children since he is reported to have had other Indian wives and lived to a ripe age of at least 80. There is an enigmatic report of a "Tessou" at Bent's Fort in Colorado in 1844, who "was in some way related to Charbenou." No last name is given to Tessou. Jean-Baptiste was also at the fort at that time. The puzzle of who Tessou was remains unsolved.[28]

Even though Grace Hebard tried to convince others that Sacajawea must have been living with Jean-Baptiste in St. Louis and that Lizette and Toussaint were Charbonneau's children by Otter Woman, there was no evidence that Sacagawea was in St. Louis or that her Toussaint was anything but a fictional character. Hebard again could not admit the obvious truth: Toussaint was Jean-Baptiste and he and his sister were adopted because their mother was dead and their father had not been heard from.

Grace Hebard had to find some evidence. Nothing concrete or documentary had turned up, so Hebard turned to oral tradition back in Wyoming. In 1905, at Wind River, she wrote to Reverend Roberts who began to recall more than the burial of Bazil's mother. He remembered talking with Agency Superintendent Dr. James Irwin in 1883; the conversation took place shortly after Reverend Roberts' arrival at Wind River. Bazil's mother, Dr. Irwin had explained to Reverend Roberts, "was with the Lewis and Clark expedition."[29] None of Dr. Irwin's Wind River documents, however, mention Sacajawea or Sacagawea or a person who was with the Lewis and Clark expedition.

Reverend Roberts also began to remember that Bazil's mother went not by the name Sacajawea but by *Wad-ze-wipe* and *Paraivo*. "I may be mistaken," he wrote to Grace Hebard, hedging a little, "but I feel confident that Sacajawea the heroine whose memory is now held in honor by the whole nation lies buried in the Indian cemetery here."[30] Before Grace Hebard contacted Roberts he only knew the old woman he had buried in 1884 as Bazil's mother. Soon after Hebard wrote to Roberts in 1905, he suddenly had three names for her.

After the Wind River Sacajawea theory had circulated around the reservation for a good ten years, a third white man added his voice to that of Reverend Roberts and James Patten. Fincelius Burnett had been the "boss farmer" hired to teach the Shoshone how to farm in the first years of the reservation. Finn Burnett was now an old pioneer, and the last days of Bazil's mother were thirty years in the past, or more. He had a lot to say about Sacajawea at Wind River.

Curiously, in a long description of Burnett's career published in an 1899 history of Wyoming by C.G. Coutant, there is no mention of his acquaintance with Sacajawea or Sacagawea.[31] Coutant's book is the first published history of the state. If Coutant had any inkling of Sacagawea at Wind River and that Burnett had known her quite well, he would have mentioned it. The logical conclusion is that Bazil's mother was never identified as Sacajawea until Grace Hebard came along in 1904.

Perhaps the most notable of Burnett's flourishes to the repertory of Wind River Sacajawea recollections is the Big Fish story. Bazil's mother (whom Burnett was now calling Sacajawea) remembered seeing a beached whale, a "big fish" at the great water, the Pacific Ocean, he said. "She went down to the coast and saw the white men and Indians cutting up the fish," he told many people. "She went over to the animal and got a portion of the fish and carried it back to the camp on her back."[32]

This is not what Clark records in his Journal. Instead, he writes that Sacagawea accompanied Clark's party to a beached whale. Nothing was left but the whale's skeleton. All of its blubber had been stripped earlier by local tribes. Clark and his party procured blubber and whale oil from those Indians.[33]

Clark's record doesn't make Finn Burnett's Big Fish story untrue. It just makes it incompatible with the historical Sacagawea. Burnett's story does not square with Clark's journal and therefore does not add to the credibility of the Wind River Sacajawea theory. Burnett himself admitted,

> It is hard to realize the migratory spirit of these Indians and the great distances traveled year after year. There are Indians here who have traveled through the mountains and deserts to the California coast, and then have returned through Oregon, Washington, and Montana.[34]

This means there were people at Wind River who had traveled the same distances as Sacagawea had with Lewis and Clark. These people would have told others about their travels to the Pacific. This is probably what Bazil's mother did.

While Reverend Roberts and James Patten had only the vaguest of memories, Finn Burnett's stories about the Wind River Sacajawea were colorful and detailed and, he said, heard from "her" own lips. Burnett described the Wind River Sacajawea as "modest in her behavior and could not easily be induced to talk."[35] Yet she apparently did talk a great deal about her various travels to Burnett and even sometimes wore a Jefferson medal said to have been received from Clark himself.

Burnett's Sacajawea stories varied with the telling and so his reliability as a witness to history is easily questioned. One of many examples is Burnett's recollections of what Bazil's mother said about Toussaint Charbonneau: in 1921, Burnett told Hebard that he had "never heard of Charbonneau, her husband."[36] Yet in 1925, Burnett said that "Sacajawea never voluntarily mentioned the name of Charbonneau."[37] Four years later, Burnett gave Hebard a sworn statement that the old woman "always spoke of Charbonneau as being a bad man who would strike her on the least provocation."[38] By 1931, Burnett was saying that she "rarely ever mentioned him in her stories of the expedition, and when she answered a question as to whether Charbonneau was with her at the time mentioned, she always spoke of him with hatred and disgust."[39]

With all this variation in oral statements and the passage of time, what Grace Hebard needed was tangible proof. If only it could be found.

There had been a manuscript of Sacajawea's memoirs, it was said. Dr. Irwin's wife Sarah had taken them down from Bazil's mother herself. No one could find the manuscript. Mrs. Irwin wasn't around to ask anymore, having died in 1888, about the same time as her husband. Variously described as a sheaf or roll of papers, the manuscript was said to have been stored by Sarah Irwin in the old adobe building that served as the Wind River Agency's office. But if you were Sarah Irwin and you had taken down the adventures of the Shoshone woman with the Lewis and Clark expedition, would you leave the manuscript at the Wind River Agency? If you were Sarah Irwin's husband and had served as Indian Agent at Wind River, wouldn't you have mentioned Sacajawea in your reports, especially since your wife had taken down her story?

The manuscript never existed. There are no disinterested secondhand accounts of it—no old diaries, no letters, or other documents telling of having read or seen or heard of the manuscript. It is said to have burned in an Agency office fire. People give two dates for when this happened: sometime in the 1880s or in 1906. In both cases, everything or most everything inside the office was said to have burned. There *was* a fire at the Agency on December 10, 1882. The log office and medicines were destroyed, but the agency employees saved the papers and books.[40]

Bazil's mother was said to have a Jefferson medal that she wore on special occasions. Medals with the impression of the president of the United States were given to Indian chiefs as a gesture of peace. Lewis and Clark set out with about 90 peace medals ranging in size from 105 mm to roughly half that for distribution to tribes they would meet up with on the journey. James Patten recalled a silver medal worn by Bazil. It had a likeness of Washington or Jefferson or maybe some other man, he said. Bazil's son Wit-to-gan had told Patten the medal had been "let" to Baptiste's son by Bazil's father.[41] This seems to indicate two different medals: one that the old woman wore and one that had been handed down from Bazil's father. Since Grace Hebard was certain that Bazil was Sacajawea's adopted son, his father would not have been Toussaint Charbonneau. But this major inconsistency didn't seem to occur to Grace Hebard. She could use the discovery of the medal to secure her reputation and provide cover for the elaborate fabrication she had constructed. The search for the medal proceeded full steam ahead.

Hebard had another trick up her sleeve. She had corresponded with John Rees, a Salmon, Idaho, writer and trader among the Lemhi, and may have persuaded him to write a long endorsement of Hebard's Wind River theory, which he sent to the Commissioner of Indian Affairs.[42] Hebard admitted that she and Rees were "coworkers"[43] but told many others that she had no influence on any investigation.

It is strange that Hebard would have sought endorsement of her theory from a trader who knew the Lemhi Shoshone, when she was intent on proving that Sacajawea was a Wyoming Shoshone who returned to her people there. Just as she had hoped, in the winter of 1925 the Bureau of Indian Affairs sent an investigator to Wind River to examine the conflicting theories about what had happened to Sacagawea. Their envoy was Dr. Charles Eastman (also known as Ohiyesa), a Sioux raised in the traditional manner. Besides his work as a homeopathic physician and advisor to presidents, Eastman had published *The Soul of an Indian* in 1911, a collection of his thoughts about Indian spirituality. Hebard claimed she had had no contact with Dr. Eastman until she received a copy of his report to the Bureau of Indian Affairs. The truth is that she fed information regularly to Dr. Eastman during and after his investigation.[44] Eastman's report, endorsed by the U.S. government, was another ploy designed to bolster the Wind River theory and Hebard cited it as proof in her book.

At Wind River, Dr. Eastman consulted mostly with Andrew Bazil, son of Bazil. The discovery of the Jefferson medal on Bazil's remains would be key evidence. But even if a Jefferson medal were found, how could one trace its origin to Sacagawea? There would be no way to prove how it was obtained, from whom, and when. Those medals did not come with serial numbers. There is no evidence that anyone asked those basic questions.

Instead, with the consent of Dick Washakie, son and successor to Chief Washakie, Superintendent Haas gave his approval to exhume Bazil's body. As a Sioux, Dr. Eastman surely knew that tribal traditions forbid digging up a body. In *The Soul of an Indian*, he wrote at length about the traditional Sioux reverence for the dead—even dead enemies—and said that so much reverence was due that it was taboo to name the dead aloud.[45]

Forty years after Dr. Eastman was at Wind River, the taboo against disturbing the remains of the dead was still very much in place. The Shoshone Business Council worried that I and my fellow anthropology graduate students would be excavating remains of the dead in Dinwoody Canyon. Remains had been monkeyed with in the 1930s as part of a government-sponsored archaeology dig. The Shoshone had never forgotten the disrespect. I do not blame them; people have violated Indian gravesites over and over and removed artifacts and put skeletons on display. We had to assure the Business Council that we were not archaeologists; we were only interested in talking with living people.

If in the 1960s the Shoshone Business Council was very concerned about the disturbance of the dead, one can only imagine that many Shoshone were deeply disturbed by the exhuming of Bazil's body in 1925. The Shoshone traditionally have a great respect for the dead and believe the body should never be touched after burial as its spirit continues to live around the remains. Most Shoshone would consider that to disturb the dead would bring misfortune.

Bazil had been buried up in the mountains and his son Andrew knew where. It is surprising that Andrew allowed his father's body to be exhumed. After all, he was a Sun Dance chief. We do not know why he gave his permission. But Dick Washakie, who had worked with Grace Hebard on a book about his father, gave his consent, as did Superintendent Haas. Finn Burnett, Haas' father-in-law, was also a witness to the exhumation. Superintendent Haas' authority was final, but it would have been illegal to exhume the body without a family member's consent, which they had from Andrew Bazil.

Grace Hebard with Dick Washakie about 1930.

Prominent white people were present at the event and all said the same thing: the Jefferson medal was not found. There was only a wallet containing illegible papers and it all crumbled to dust.

Many years later, Rupert Weeks, a widely known Shoshone story-teller and the namesake of the Shoshone Cultural Center at Wind River, told me how he had always had great doubts about the Wind River Saca-jawea story. He said he would only believe it if the medal had been found. But the medal was not found and he didn't believe the story was true. Another Shoshone elder, also a skeptic, told me that Dr. Eastman's main informant and son of Bazil, Andrew Bazil, was *dee-vee-jee ishump*, a very great liar. It is possible that Andrew Bazil feared great misfortune and even death for allowing his father's body to be dug up.

Bazil's remains were taken from the mountains and reburied next to his mother's purported grave in the mission cemetery. Baptiste's remains were never placed there.

In recent years another piece of tangible evidence has gained prominence over the medal that was never found. Some say Sacajawea saved a sand dollar she found on a Pacific beach. She saved the sand dollar for many years, bringing it with her to Wind River, finally presenting it to Chief Washakie. It is said that you can see the sand dollar for yourself in the neckerchief holder Washakie wore in several photographs. But sand dollars crumble easily. When you see them on the beach, they are usually in fragments. It is unusual to find a whole, intact sand dollar. No sand dollar would have survived that long under those conditions of travel and would never have been strong enough to be used as a neckerchief holder. Even if you could find a sand dollar that had belonged to Chief Washakie, it would be impossible to prove who gave it to him.

But today the legend of the sand dollar is cast in bronze. Bud Boller's 2003 Sacajawea statue in the Sacajawea Cemetery shows her walking on a Pacific Ocean beach. In her left hand Sacajawea lifts up her skirt and with her right hand she holds a large round object poised between her fingers—the sand dollar.

## Chapter 6

# Radio Waves
# over the Grave

In the early 1920s, Lander lawyer Porter B. Coolidge represented two women running cattle on the reservation. During a four-year period, the women continued to allow their cattle to trespass and refused to pay some of the grazing fees. Coolidge attempted to negotiate a compromise payment of $7,100, one-half the full amount and an enormous sum in those days.[1] At the same time he was collecting attorney's fees for representing two women who were cheating the Shoshone, Coolidge wanted to use Sacajawea to boost tourism in Lander. In both cases, monetary gain seems to have been the sole motive

Coolidge also wrote lyrics. During the period in which he represented the two women, he wrote a song with an Englishman named Frederic Boothroyd. They called the song "Sacajawea." The last verse goes like this:

> Now sunset's golden dreams are dead,
> The Indian girl from he hath fled;
> Still linger in the starlit skies,
> The dusk and splendor of her eyes
> And voice of distant waterfall
> Sweet echoes of her song recall,
> Sweet echoes of her song recall.[2]

The song is a funeral dirge, minor key and low register, tom-tom beats played on a low B. Coolidge's lyrics sexualize Sacajawea, giving her youth, long hair, and mysterious eyes. In the other verses, so alive is she for the singer that he picks a rose for her. But Sacajawea cannot take the rose. She is dead, the companion of the twilight sleep of death and dead dreams.

The Wind River Sacajawea could hardly have been the inspiration for the song, as the legend's entire point is that she died a very old woman. Instead, Coolidge based his lyrics on a common stereotype: the Indian Princess. A native beauty, the Princess is sympathetic to the white man's mission to civilize Native peoples. The Indian Princess is strictly a European notion that had no bearing on the life of the real Sacagawea. We don't know if Sacagawea was the daughter of a chief or not, but even if she had been, she would not have been a princess because daughters of chiefs were not a form of nobility in North America. In the Southeast, some of the Native societies were ranked, with chiefs, nobles, and commoners. Chieftainship among western tribes, such as the Shoshone, was based on merit and achievement earned in one's lifetime. It was not an inherited title.

Consider the historical Sacagawea. Captured as a young girl in a raid, she was sold or gambled to a much older French Canadian trader. Toussaint Charbonneau was not her husband; he was her master. Theirs was a master–slave relationship. Sacagawea was also valuable to the Lewis and Clark expedition. The expedition needed her, both as a speaker of Shoshone and as a token that the expedition was not a war party. By the time the expedition reached Shoshone country, it was clear that Sacagawea and her baby could guarantee safe passage and help obtain the horses the expedition needed to cross the Rockies.

Contrast this reality with the romanticized Wind River Sacajawea. Instead of an analysis of the motivations of Lewis and Clark, we hear only of Sacajawea's heroism and her devotion to the expedition's success. Sacajawea is elevated into the guide of the expedition. In the hands of Grace Hebard, the Wind River Sacajawea becomes an independent, self-sufficient presuffragette and rugged feminist who prevails against all odds without any support from a kin group, finally rejecting Toussaint Charbonneau, escaping into Comanche country, and returning—without a husband and on her own—to Wind River to be cared for by her adopted son, Bazil. In the 19th century, it would have been almost unthinkable for a Native woman to have separated herself willingly from kindred for an extended period of time.

Coolidge's idea was to broadcast his song "Sacajawea" over the radio from stations in Portland and St. Louis, the two most distant points of the Lewis and Clark expedition. The radio waves carrying "weird strains of the Indian song" would meet over Sacajawea's grave in the mission cemetery at Wind River,[3] which, since 1909, had a concrete pedestal with a bronze plaque, paid for by another white lawyer, Timothy Burke.

Still, P. B. Coolidge was a local booster, not content to memorialize Sacajawea with a mere song. In 1923, he wrote to Grace Hebard. He had seen an article in a Chicago newspaper about how South Dakota, site of

Fort Manuel Lisa where Sacagawea had died in 1812, was trying to "wrest" Sacajawea from Wyoming. He wondered what could be done about it.[4] Coolidge proposed a monument to Sacajawea to be put up at the head of Lander's Main Street where every tourist going to the great south entrance to Yellowstone Park would see it. The Lander statue was to match that of Buffalo Bill in Cody at the great eastern entrance to the park. Coolidge enlisted the support of the First National Bank, Lander, and thought the monument should cost $50,000; ten times the $5,000 request introduced by United States Senator Warren of Wyoming.[5] Fifty thousand dollars was the equivalent of $500,000 today.

The U.S. government never appropriated money for the statue, probably because there was serious contention over whether it should be in South Dakota or Wyoming. Outside of Wyoming, the Wind River theory was in trouble. Luttig's journal had been published. Brackenridge's journal had been published. It was becoming very clear that Sacagawea had died at Fort Manuel Lisa in 1812. A growing number of historians were demanding that Grace Hebard produce better evidence to support her Wind River Sacajawea.

By this time, the marker dedicated to Sacajawea had been in place at Wind River about 15 years. Descendants of Bazil and Baptiste had been told by Dr. Grace Hebard and Reverend Roberts that they were descendants of Sacajawea, and by now some actually believed it. The white authority structure had told them so. And now they told their children and their grandchildren that the family came from Sacajawea.

Some came not to believe. As a summer school student at the University of Wyoming, Irtense Large, a granddaughter of Bazil, became known as a great-granddaughter of Sacajawea. She presented a paper on her illustrious ancestor for the history department. Already a rural school teacher in the Green River area, Large recited her ancestry exactly as Grace Hebard had constructed it for her.[6] But in later years, Irtense Large Enos said she no longer believed in the Wind River Sacajawea theory.[7]

Some lived their whole lives believing. By 1925, Bernice and Esther "Essie" Burnett, self-styled great-great-granddaughters of the Wind River Sacajawea, posed for a photograph with a great-great-grandnephew of Meriwether Lewis.[8] Hebard's theory would make them great-great-great-grandnieces, as they were descended from Bazil/Pa:si. Thirty years later, Essie, as she was known, was still posing for photographs as a descendant of Sacajawea, but now as the North Dakota representative on the occasion of the 150th anniversary of the Lewis and Clark expedition, which had wintered in that State. In fact, many North Dakotans believed that the historical Sacagawea was Hidatsa, a North Dakota native. The large artificial lake created on their reservation in the 1950s was named Lake Sakakawea. None of the conflicting information about Sacajawea's true roots seemed to matter to Essie. In spite of Essie's belief that Sacajawea had returned to Wyoming and was originally from Idaho, she participated as the representative of North Dakota. As an old woman, Essie admitted that she had heard that the woman with Lewis and Clark had died in 1812 at Fort Manuel Lisa. But Essie still held on to what her parents had told her: she was descended from Sacajawea. That was enough for her.[9] Her sister, Bernice Twitchell of Wind River, continued to be a strong advocate for the Wind River Sacajawea.

By the 1920s, Americans were ripe for a change in their image of the Indian from that of the barbaric, blood-thirsty savage. The Indian Princess was still alive and well, but she was a woman. Women had not been warriors, generally speaking, and so could be romanticized. But now, the frontier had ended and so had the Indian wars. Gone were the days of bloody massacres. Indians had been completely defeated and now lived on reservations.

The United States had begun to look at Indians in a new way. Like it or not, they were part of the historical fabric of the country. In 1924, Congress granted all Indians the right of citizenship, long overdue. Those who advocated citizenship cited the large number of Indians who fought in World War I. The Indians had actually helped us win a war. They had fought on our side, instead of being enemies of the United States.

In the early 1950s, when I was a boy, the revised image of the Indian was well in place. The radio Indian I remember was a loyal, trusted helper. Children still played cowboys and Indians. We put on our holsters and played target practice with our cap guns, miniature six shooters. Sometimes the cowboys won, sometimes the Indians—we tried to be fair. At home after school, we listened to a host of popular radio programs starring heroic sheriffs like Tom Mix and stoic Indians like Tonto, the "faithful companion" of the Lone Ranger, or Straight Arrow, the "honest Indian." The radio Indian kept his word. He existed to help the white man, not defeat him. If you had asked me back then to describe an Indian, the first word to come to my mind would have been *trustworthy*. Everyone knew Indians kept their word.

We kids had little idea that whites had forcibly stolen land and subsistence from the Indians. We didn't know that tuberculosis had run rampant through the tribes with the bacilli passed among family members who lived in crowded, unsanitary conditions. We didn't know that Indians had starved and that the government had cheated them out of land, broken every treaty, and owed them money.

In school, we learned that Indians were peaceful and spiritually minded people who lived a simple hunting-gathering or horticultural way of life. The peaceful Pueblo Indians of New Mexico were the archetypal example.

In our Boy Scout, Girl Scout, and Campfire Girl troops we learned that Indians were Nature's Children. Because they depended on the natural world for survival and had no need for the industrial way of life, they were somehow purer and more spiritually minded than whites.[10] Our modern world needed a new model of conduct that Indian culture could provide, the notion went. Technology, national rivalry, and ethnic hatred had caused the death of millions in World Wars I and II—destruction on a scale never before seen. Social changes brought about by the automobile and the tensions between older agrarian and newer industrial ways of life made escape into nature seem even more attractive. Americans romanticized the Indian as "the other"—the opposite of their own acquisitive culture.

Craft and curio industries and staged dances for tourists could not provide Indians with a livelihood and only put human beings on display. Furthermore, the Shoshone at Wind River didn't begin to receive much income from the oil and gas discovered on their reservation until the 1940s. Maud Clairmont, a Shoshone businesswoman and member of the Tribal Council, told me the United States government withheld 50 percent of tribal income from distribution as monthly per capita checks for many years, believing that a fund had to be created of surplus assets. Maud and other Tribal Council members lobbied to allow distribution of 85 percent of the income, explaining that Indians needed it to survive. Even now, the United States still withholds 15 percent of tribal income.

Even in the 1970s, many Shoshone were living mostly on surplus commodities like white flour, white sugar, cheese, peanut butter, and lard. More substantial foods appeared only seasonally. Meat came from fall hunting and fishing, while fruit and vegetables came from wild sources or family gardens. Parents sent their children to the Fort Washakie Day School because they knew they'd get a good meal there. The school was known to the kids as Gravy High.

The paternalism and power of the Bureau of Indian Affairs was often painful to witness. Many times I drove Tom Wesaw to the Wind River Indian Agency office to inquire about the status of rent payments due on land he leased out and when he could expect the next payments. Sometimes there was no money because rental fees had not been collected. Sometimes there was no money because the bureaucracy was slow in processing payments. Tom Wesaw, a respected man who was more than 80 years old, was not allowed to collect rent without going through the agency. The United States government technically owned and managed all allotments because the federal government holds the land in trust for the Indians.

The allotment system came about because it was thought Indians couldn't manage their own property. The United States sometimes referred to Indians as "children" in treaties; certainly, Indians were understood to be wards of the government. The General Allotment Act of 1887, also known as the Dawes Act, gave each Indian nuclear family a certain amount of land. How much land that was depended on the arability and irrigation of the land. It was a terrible mistake to move families that had hunted buffalo only a few years earlier onto small family-operated farms and ranches without offering to help them establish a means to buy and sell their animals and farm products, such as forming a buying cooperative, a marketing cooperative, or a tribal cattle ranching operation.

Successful ranching at Wind River depended from the beginning on access to irrigated land to provide supplies of fodder and range land. Both were in short supply, and the successful farmers and ranchers were usually Shoshone of mixed ancestry who leased allotments and amassed capital to purchase other holdings. By mid-20th century, this group of ranchers constituted the Shoshone middle class, and rose to leadership positions on the Business Council.

By the time I first came to Wind River in 1966, most of the allotments made to individual families 60 years earlier had become unproductive as sources of income or subsistence.[11] People told how the Shoshone used to raise cattle and grain and maintain large gardens in earlier years. For the most part, that was no longer true. Many of the farms had corrals for cattle that were empty and falling down. As for a cooperative cattle operation, the Eastern Shoshone never had one. The large cattle ranches, mostly in the Big Wind River area, were and are owned by families whose ancestry is mostly white; they lease land from others who are mostly Shoshone.[12]

The Allotment Act of 1887 was a big mistake and mistakes are difficult to admit, especially by those in power. It's been much easier to romanticize the old way of life of the Indians. If Americans really knew life on the reservation, they might understand what it's like to be a conquered people. Instead, romantic accounts like Eva Emery Dye's *The Conquest* and Grace Hebard's *Sacajawea: Guide and Interpreter of Lewis and Clark* seized public imagination. It did not matter that there was no proven connection between Sacagawea and the Wind River Shoshone. It did not matter that the professional historians said Sacagawea had been a Lemhi Shoshone or that her name was Hidatsa or that she had died at Fort Manuel Lisa in 1812 or that no document mentioned her at Wind River.

Whatever the reasons, Grace Hebard could not let her theory die, could not give in to the historians, particularly those from the Dakotas whom she saw as her archrivals. And so in 1932 Hebard set about not only publishing a book based on her article written two decades before but securing an impressive and permanent memorial to Sacajawea in the cemetery at Wind River. The cemetery, now newly named after Sacajawea, was to become the focal point of the visible and concrete imagery demonstrating to all that Sacajawea had lived at Wind River and had died there.

*Chapter 7*

# A Big Mouth
# and a Pink Chevrolet

*Blanche's living room, Lander, July 1980*

"My grandfather would *never* have told a lie. He knew Sacajawea and heard her speak at the Great Treaty." Maud was pointing her finger at Blanche Schroer.

For many years, Maud Clairmont had been on the Shoshone Business Council. She was used to defending the Wind River Sacajawea to anyone who would listen. Besides, Maud never took a backseat to anyone. She was proud of her mixed Indian and European heritage. Her father was part Sioux and part French; on her mother's side, Maud was Salish, Iroquois, and Shoshone. Maud's family had lived at Wind River since the very beginning of the reservation. Of that, too, Maud was proud.

A very honest and devout Catholic, Maud ran a small motel on her deeded land on the reservation. The property shouldered Highway 287 and had a couple of gas pumps. I stayed at her motel a number of times over a 20-year period. There were occasions when she didn't charge me for staying. Her husband had died the year after I arrived at Wind River, and she seemed to enjoy my company. Maud was always kind, generous, and willing to talk with just about anybody. If Maud liked you, lots of other people liked you, too. Maud liked me.

Blanche was white, born in Iowa, the daughter of the reservation's physician. A relative newcomer, Blanche had "only" lived in the area a mere five decades. As young women in the 1930s, Blanche and Maud had worked together at Matt McGuire's trading post at Fort Washakie.

I met Blanche for the first time at the Nu Way Café in Lander. She was seated at the next table and we got to talking about this and that. A

51

cup of coffee or two later it clicked! This glamorous older blonde at the next table was the woman I'd heard people talk about in town and on the reservation.

In a way, Blanche Schroer was tougher than anyone I'd met. It was a good kind of toughness, the kind that left Blanche open to finding answers for herself. In the 1950s she'd asked if she could attend peyote meetings of the Native American Church. The Shoshone had welcomed her and had been happy to share their religious ceremony with a non-Indian they knew. It was very unusual at the time for a woman, especially a white woman, to be invited to a peyote meeting. It only showed that the Shoshone trusted her. Blanche returned the favor in the form of an article for *The Denver Post*. She wrote it to dispel the superstitious myths that peyote is a harmful drug that destroys minds.

Ever since the first time I heard people talking around town about Blanche, I admired her spunk, her nerve, and her verve. As I came to know Blanche better, I found her to be open-minded but also guarded. She had good reason to be wary. She had met with a lot of local criticism for one of her other great interests: Sacajawea, or as Blanche called her, Sac. Blanche had started out as a true believer in the Wind River story. Then she began to read about Sac. A lot. Blanche was an amateur historian and later won the Western Writers of America Spur Award.[1]

As she tried to put the pieces of the Sac puzzle together and found they didn't really fit, Blanche made a very Blanche move. She went right to the source, right to the oldest Shoshone she knew, Jenny Martinez. Blanche asked point blank exactly the question that was bothering her: *had Jenny known Paraivo? If so, had Paraivo ever said anything about being with Lewis and Clark?*

The answers she got surprised her. It was not what she had read in Grace Hebard's book that everyone always pointed to. Yes, Jenny Martinez told Blanche. She had known Paraivo. She had lived around Paraivo for many years, but she had never heard her talk about being with Lewis and Clark.[2]

Paraivo and Sac were not the same person, of that Blanche was now convinced. But Blanche did not research Paraivo. What bothered her was how the legend had come to be. And as she learned about Grace Hebard and the handful of local whites who had backed her up, Blanche became more and more determined to set the record straight.

To throw down the gauntlet locally, Blanche had the Lander newspaper reprint a rhetorically charged article she had written about Sac for *In Wyoming*, a booster magazine for the state.[3] It was a move designed to provoke comment.

And plenty of comment there was. Some Landerites accused Blanche of inventing stories. They accused her of destroying the credibility of the informants Grace Hebard quoted in her book *Sacajawea*. Some of the informants were parents or grandparents. It had become personal.

One of those who took it personally was Maud. Her grandfather Edmo LeClair had been one of Grace Hebard's informants. Maud told me that she was convinced that her grandfather had told the truth. Blanche, her one-time friend, was therefore not telling the truth.

For Blanche, too, the Wind River Sacajawea had its personal side. She had an axe to grind that had nothing to do with Sac. Blanche's brother Joe had run a seedy package-goods store—meaning a liquor store—on the reservation. The Business Council, of which Maud was a member, had shut him down. Blanche also had acrimonious ties to the family of Reverend John Roberts. Blanche's brother had been married to one of Reverend Roberts' granddaughters. The marriage had ended badly.

Blanche herself was the financially independent widow of a successful appliance dealer in Lander, which meant that in this conservative small town, she could pretty much thumb her nose at people she disagreed with. Blanche had the courage of her convictions and the western swagger to go with them. Her money meant that no one could silence her.

Quite a gal, the last of the flappers, western style. Blonde and beautiful even into her 80s, tooling around town in her pink Chevrolet, trumpeting what she thought was good and right about the Shoshone, straightening out the Sacajawea boosters.

As the waters calmed after the appearance of her article in the Lander newspaper, Blanche asked me if I could arrange for her to talk with Maud. It was to be a reconciliation of old friends, she told me.

I hesitated. But one day, Maud began to reminisce about her son who had died in a tragic accident and how he and his sister had known Blanche's son. I decided the time had come to ask Maud to meet with Blanche. If Blanche and Maud couldn't agree, maybe they could reach some kind of understanding.

The day of reconciliation arrived. Now Blanche sat back in her emerald green velvet sofa. She bit her lower lip and waited.

I waited, too, my eyes wandering from Maud, angrier than I had ever seen her, to the hard black lacquer of Blanche's Chinese coffee table.

"You had no business saying that Sacajawea was a hoax in that newspaper article," Maud said at last. Her words were cold and exact.

Blanche drew in her lips. She had to know Maud's only recent information about Sac came from Blanche's own article. Who was Maud going to believe—her own grandparents or Blanche? Of course, Maud was simply going to repeat what her grandparents had told her years before. They were good, honest people, Edmo and Philesette LeClair. Successful, hard-working ranchers, staunch populists and proud of their

Indian heritage. Like everyone on the reservation, Maud respected her grandparents and their deep roots in the Shoshone soil.

"But Maud, let me explain," Blanche tried. "There's another side to the story."

"I don't care. My grandfather said that Sacajawea was present at the signing of the Great Treaty. What more evidence could anyone want?"

I saw by the look on Blanche's face that she knew it was useless to continue. It was time for me to take Maud to lunch.

At the Nu Way Café, Maud held her menu. She was shaking with anger.

"How dare she," Maud hissed. "She insults the Shoshone people and my grandfather. She's no Shoshone and yet she plays as though she knows more than we do."

I had no answer for this. I was in the same position as Blanche, although at the time I knew almost nothing about the woman with Lewis and Clark and the conflicting theories about her life. All I could do was listen to Maud as a friend. Her fight with Blanche underscored for me the enormous emotional investment on both sides.

It wasn't for another few weeks that I ran into Blanche again. She handed me a copy of the article that had appeared in the Lander newspaper.

"The worst thing is," Blanche told me, "I know most of those people on the reservation and in town haven't even read the article. They don't want to read it."

"Why?" I asked.

"They don't want to know the truth. They think they already know it. It's a done deal."

It wasn't a done deal for only the Shoshone. In town, Blanche's most vocal enemy was a white woman named Minnie Woodring. Mrs. Woodring took the fight to a local newspaper. She wrote a series on Sacajawea, relying heavily on testimony from a granddaughter of the old boss farmer, Finn Burnett.[4] The argument in Woodring's articles was the same as Maud's: my grandfather said it was so and therefore, it was so. To disagree is to dishonor my family.

In my own family, family history has also been emotional. My great-uncle was a local history buff in a small town in Minnesota. He always told us that we were descended from Alexander Hamilton, as his grandmother's maiden name had been Hamilton and she came from back east. For years, nobody doubted the story. I happened to research our family's history and discovered there was no connection to Alexander Hamilton, even though our Hamilton ancestors came from back east, too, but from Connecticut, not New York.

Had my uncle deliberately lied? I don't think so. He was trying to piece together our family history from little bits of information that had been told to him. The pieces seemed to fit, but actually, they did not. My uncle built himself up a little with the story because he told it to his local history cronies and to relatives. Many people have done exactly the same thing. Anthropologist Margaret Mead once told me, "We all have ancestors who had castles in Wales."[5]

Finn Burnett, the old boss farmer at Wind River, reminds me of my uncle. Burnett provided some of the most important oral testimony to shore up the Wind River Sacajawea. The Burnett family had a stake in the Wind River Sacajawea theory for this reason. But there was another reason, too: his youngest son, Fincelius Jr., had married a granddaughter of Pa:si. Now Finn's family could claim a blood link to Sacajawea. And today some of Finn Burnett's many descendants claim that connection. For example, Essie Burnett Horne, the woman who led the caravan during the 150th anniversary celebration of the Lewis and Clark expedition certainly claimed the connection. Essie's cousin, Milward Simpson, former governor of Wyoming, United States senator, and the father of former Senator Alan Simpson, was very vocal in his support of the Wind River Sacajawea.

It was this kind of family interest that infuriated Blanche Schroer. The important thing, she felt, was the truth. It didn't matter who you stepped on or whose grandparents you insulted to tell it. The occasion or mood didn't matter, so long as the truth prevailed.

As early as 1963, Blanche was pointing her finger in accusation. She was at the unveiling of the monument erected by the DAR in the Sacajawea Cemetery—there to tell reporters that the Wind River Sacajawea was a lie.

Locally, Blanche was a lone voice. Nationally, professional historians had been discrediting the Wyoming theory since the 1920s. But nobody in Lander or Wind River read the historians' accounts or even knew that there was another camp. If they did, they kept quiet. Blanche Schroer was in Lander, on the spot, and vocal.

For her part, Blanche enjoyed the notoriety. She was frustrated but there was a kind of adrenaline high to it. She still played bridge with her old friends, but now she had a certain reputation. When she drove down the street in her pink Chevrolet, people pointed at her. *You can shoot all the bullets you want at me*, she seemed to always be saying, *but I'll never recant.*

People on the reservation were talking. They started saying something I hadn't heard before: that the woman who had died in South Dakota in 1812 was not Sacajawea but Charbonneau's other woman, Otter Woman. That and their grandparents' words ended the matter, they said. No further discussion was necessary.

# Chapter 8

# The Clue in
# the Sun Dance

It was 1966. The Vietnam conflict had escalated into a major war. Surprisingly, the national media were paying a lot of attention just then to an 80-year-old Shoshone Sun Dance chief named Tom Wesaw. "Chief" is the English term given to the leader of the Sun Dance, who "puts it up" because he has had a vision of what it should mean and do. Wesaw had asked the tribe if he could sponsor a Sun Dance to end the war and also to pray for the men in combat, both Indian and non-Indian. By this time, there were 500,000 American troops in Vietnam. The war was on everyone's mind.

I was on the point of having to make a decision about Vietnam: comply with the draft, enlist, or resist. I'd arrived at Wind River for the first time only two weeks before, a young man of 23. The Sun Dance, the most important event in the Shoshone ceremonial year, was to take place very soon. The Shoshone kept telling me it was difficult and challenging. Only a couple of white guys had ever "gone into" the Sun Dance, as they say. White skin isn't as tough, they explained. It's thin and soft. I might have a more difficult time than an Indian would. I might not withstand the rigors of the Sun Dance.

The Shoshone Sun Dance is not like that of the Lakota Sioux who pierce chest muscles, make flesh offerings, and drag a buffalo skull tied to thongs laced through the back muscles. But the Shoshone dance is just as physically demanding. It is a fast—no food or water for three days—with singing, continuous dancing, and prayers for power and healing. It usually takes place in July or August when the heat is most intense at Wind River, often reaching 100 degrees or more.

57

Dance lodge. I memorized the general expectations and sequences laid out in the booklet.

The modern Sun Dance ceremony takes place between Thursday evening and the following Sunday afternoon so participants don't miss much work. On Thursday night, the dancers form a long line at sunset and circle the lodge four times before filing into the lodge behind the chief and his assistant and taking their places inside the perimeter. Dancers wear nothing above the waist but an eagle-bone whistle and an ermine pelt around the neck. On their index fingers are eagle down feathers held between the thumb and index fingers. The dancers take a bed-roll and a sheet into the Sun Dance Lodge. The sheet is to cover the body and prevent sunburn when the dancer rests.

Usually two brothers, cousins, or friends will enter together and take turns so that one of them is always dancing. The dancing is strenuous, involving a hopping step back and forth from one's place on the edge of the interior of the lodge to the center pole where the head of a buffalo hangs. As the dancers go back and forth, they blow on their whistles to the heavy rhythm of drums and traditional Sun Dance songs. Soon deep furrows develop in the earth of the Sun Dance lodge, paths where each dancer moves to and from the center pole.

But dancers must rest. Friends and relatives provide a cool bed of cattails and give sweet sage and peppermint to smell. Even during the hottest time of the day, there are always a few men dancing. It is important to maintain the continuity of the dance at all times.

Each day there is a morning prayer service. A quiet time follows; dancers can visit, inhale healing cedar incense over a pit inside the entrance to the lodge, and talk quietly. They may even leave the lodge to relieve themselves and talk to relatives and friends.

Then the dancing begins again. The cycle of dance and worship and rest repeats itself over and over. But on the afternoon of the third and last day, there is a change. Anyone from the community who wants a blessing stands before the center pole to be brushed with eagle feathers by the Sun Dance chief and his assistant. Dozens of Shoshone, even some in walkers or wheelchairs, come forward. The chief prays a long prayer asking Dam Apë for assistance. Finally all the dancers line up for the last blessings and prayers. With a cup of water, the fast is broken and the Sun Dance ends.

I learned all this information by heart and looked forward to the beginning of Tom Wesaw's Sun Dance with a mixture of fear and anticipation. I was wearing my skirt made from satin. It was bright and expensive-looking. I wrapped the wide beaded belt around my waist. My ermine pelt, eagle feathers, and whistle were in place. Without these things, I could never have hoped to participate in the Sun Dance. Two fellow grad students promised to help the St. Clair family gather cattails for my bed and give me moral support.

Tom Johnson in a Shoshone Sun Dance, 1967.

I was ready to go into the Sun Dance now. Still, of course, I knew that the three-day fast, with dancing in the hot sun, was going to be very difficult. It would be an endurance test.

The first day was the hardest. The prospect of having no liquids for the next two days of dancing in the sun was one thing, but the constant glare of the High Plains afternoon sun and the threat of severe sunburn began to frighten me. I tan easily but the more I danced, the more my skin was exposed to the sun. At a mile high, the sun is more intense. I had to choose between dancing a great deal and exposing my skin or lying on my bedroll, covered by a sheet. I knew I could not allow myself to get severely sunburned so I tended to dance in the shadows when the sun shone on the opposite side of the lodge.

By the second day, as we all lost body fluids, we became lighter and dancing became easier. A group of assistants drove slender saplings into the rocky soil in front of each dancer's place and painted the saplings yellow, the chiefly color. It helped to hold on to the saplings to steady ourselves. The hot sun and the total absence of water made the mouth feel as though it were stuffed with cotton. Endurance was part of the sacrificial side of the dance.

Before daybreak, all thirty-five of us rose from our bedrolls to form a line in the middle of the lodge. We faced the rising sun. With eagle bone whistles and eagle down feathers held out, we greeted the sun until it had risen well above the horizon. Then we gathered in a large circle in front of the entrance to the lodge, placing blankets over our heads and singing songs in response to the prayers of Tom Wesaw and his son, George. Just as I had read in the pamphlet, a large number of spectators formed outside the entrance on Sunday. They bowed their heads as Tom Wesaw and George prayed. Later that morning, the dancing reached a new level of intensity in preparation for the community healing service. We were really pushing ourselves to lend support to Tom Wesaw and George and the purpose of the ceremony. They came up to each one of us and brushed our bodies from head to foot with eagle feathers and took up soil from *sogop bia*—Mother Earth—and touched the whole body with it.

Occasionally, a dancer will hyperventilate, especially on the final day as dancing gets more intense, and receive a vision. After the ceremony, people asked me if I had had a vision. No, not that kind, I answered, but I told them that I came to realize that the Sun Dance was not about worshipping the sun but about receiving help and blessings from the great Power in the universe that the sun represents, a power that can be used by us poor creatures on earth to improve and examine our lives and help us become less selfish. The prayers taught me those things. Through the dance, this great Power can be transferred to living human beings where it can work wonders. But I began to wonder how the ceremony began, who brought it to the Shoshone, and what kind of person might have done that.

I did make it through three hot, exhausting days and nights. Thirty pounds of mostly water melted off my lanky 23-year-old frame. I now had a much better sense of who I was, of courage, of the importance of my life, of what I might be able to teach others. I did not know how my questions about military service would be answered, but I had an idea that there was a strength and power out there—and maybe there were other people—that would help me.

I was baptized and confirmed in a Christian church. I attended services almost all my adult life and have raised my children as Christians. But no single event in my religious upbringing prepared me for the transforming experience of the Shoshone Sun Dance. In any kind of scriptural tradition, religious people must make an honest effort to apply the writings of prophets and visionaries who lived hundreds of years ago to present circumstances. This is not easy. In the Sun Dance, the meaning of social concerns and responsibilities becomes immediate. The purpose of the ceremony changes with its leader, yet in every ceremony all the people receive tangible blessings and stand before the entire community as witnesses to its transforming power. It would be hard to think of the Sun Dance as an empty formula that could never move a dancer to examine his life. I can easily understand why many Shoshone Christians also worship in the Sun Dance.

Tom Wesaw must have anticipated this. Several days after the ceremony he gave me his blessing and one of his Sun Dance whistles, a symbolic transfer of power and token of esteem. All these years later, I still uncover this whistle when I need help.

The summer following Tom Wesaw's ceremony, Johnny Trehero and his Crow Indian assistant allowed me to dance in their Sun Dance. Shoshone tradition has it that in the early 1800s Ohamagwaya, a great-grandfather of Johnny, brought the Sun Dance to the Shoshone from the Comanche.[2] Johnny took the Shoshone Sun Dance to the Crow in about 1941.[3] Taking a ceremony to another tribe has happened several times in the past. The Wind River Sun Dance now has several offspring. You can find it among the Fort Hall Shoshone, three different Ute groups and, of course, the Crow.

The purpose of Johnny's Sun Dance was entirely different from that of Tom Wesaw's. Tom's vision was about the war; Johnny wanted to create closer relations between the Shoshone and the Crow. His Sun Dances were all about reaching out to other tribes and building alliances.

Johnny had a great sense of humor. The Sun Dance is a serious matter but Johnny was in a direct line of descent of Sun Dance Chiefs. He had spiritual gifts and that perhaps allowed his jovial personality to shine through. Right before his Sun Dance, he rode around the Sun Dance field on a horse, stopping to joke with people. It was part of Johnny's style and reminded me of his Indian name, *Babaro*—buffalo rendered in English by a Shoshone boy.

In the decades after I danced in Johnny's Sun Dance, I witnessed many others, although I never danced again. I couldn't tell you how many Sun Dances I've seen, sponsored by different Shoshone for different purposes. But it wasn't until the summer of 2003 that I began to understand the link between the Shoshone Sun Dance and the true identity of the Wind River Sacajawea.

# Chapter 9

# Paraivo, Chief Woman

In the summer of 2003, a Wind River Shoshone friend invited me to join him at Bannock Creek on the Fort Hall Shoshone reservation near Pocatello, Idaho. From Wind River, it's a drive of about 300 miles west over several mountain ranges. We were to attend the Sun Dance together.

I'd wanted to visit this ceremony for a long time. It is different from the Sun Dance at Wind River in two very important ways: at Bannock Creek women may dance and they may also act as Sun Dance chiefs. The women are equal to the men in spiritual power.

But first I needed to talk with Daisy St. Clair. She and her husband Herman had helped me when I first came to Wind River, loaning me that booklet about the Sun Dance and special clothing. They'd given me moral support, too.

A good 30 years had passed since I last saw Daisy. She was in her 90s by now and a widow. I had heard old age had taken Daisy's eyesight but that her mind was still alert. Daisy had spent her girlhood at Fort Hall; if anyone at Wind River knew about how women came to be Sun Dance leaders at Fort Hall, it would be Daisy.

I phoned her home and asked her son Orville if she would mind answering some questions about the Sun Dance. He hesitated a moment, mentioning his mother's age and condition. He invited me to visit their ranch home on North Fork. Maybe Daisy would be up to my visit, maybe not, he said.

This was how I arranged to talk to most of my informants at Wind River. My informants and I already know each other or a friend or relative recommended me. I call people, identify myself as an anthropologist, tell them I want to talk to them about some topic, and ask if I can visit them. If they consent, I set up an appointment. If they choose not to talk to me, I thank them politely and never bother them again. Sometimes I pick up information casually at a social gathering like a pow-wow. Sometimes this information provides a lead to a more formal interview. I never buy informants drinks, never bring a six-pack to an interview to loosen an informant's tongue, never pay an informant. I suppose you could justify paying for people's time—and I did pay the Shoshone who gave me language lessons—but information should not come with strings attached. Money can be a form of pressure, especially if those extra dollars will help you make it to the end of the month. People shouldn't be pressured to give out information.

And there is another reason I never pay informants. I don't want the relationship I build with them to rest on money. I always consider them friends first, although they know I am an anthropologist. The information Shoshone have shared with me over the years has been freely and willingly given.

Grace Hebard's method of interviewing informants involved payments of money, or payments of grapes or an orange from the local trading post. Working with an interpreter, whom she also paid, she often freely inserted names. After a discussion involving the woman the Shoshone knew as Paraivo, she inserted Sacajawea and several other names for her obtained from John Rees, the Lemhi trader. Many statements from informants were recorded as sworn affidavits, with witnesses, in order to bolster the impression that Paraivo had been with Lewis and Clark, and had to be Sacajawea. The oldest Shoshone informants only told stories about how Paraivo was with the first white men, spoke at the 1868 Treaty, or brought the Sun Dance to the Shoshone—all of which were undoubtedly true. But the insertions about Lewis and Clark may have been told to some informants long before they were interviewed; by the time Hebard interviewed them in the 1920's, years had passed since rumors were first spread about Bazil's mother being Sacajawea.

Sometimes, informants talk for a while—years, even—then decide to stop talking. Norbert Blackwood worked with me for many years. He doesn't have a phone so I drove out to his ranch to find him. This time, he didn't answer my knock on the door.

There were noises of someone moving around inside the house. Norbert's pickup was in the driveway. I folded my arms across my chest and leaned against the side of Norbert's house, thinking that it had been several years since we'd talked. Maybe Norbert had grown hard of hearing. Maybe I should knock again, and louder.

Across the way, the front door of his son's house opened. He came out, hands cupped around a morning mug of coffee.

"Dad's left town," he called. "He went to pick up a horse in Montana."

I nodded. "I'm sorry to have missed him," I said.

And I was. Next time I come out, I'll try to reach Norbert again—but not for an interview and not as an anthropologist. I'm an old-timer now and I'd like to chat about friends we knew many years ago.

It was early evening when I arrived at the St. Clair's. A late-afternoon thundershower had matted the earth and stirred up the scent of sage. Orville was playing ball with his sons in the front. I squinted against the pink rim of setting sun along the mountains and waved to him.

Daisy was waiting for me in her living room. The same laughter lines at her eyes, the same quick smile. She put out a hand and something swelled in my throat. She had been so kind to me all those years ago.

Daisy had a lot to tell me. Her voice and memory were still strong.

"The first woman Sun Dance chief was Paparosa about the time of the first World War," she said. "Paparosa told everyone she would put up a Sun Dance so that the young Shoshone and Bannock men who didn't want to go to war wouldn't have to. Paparosa's vision had power. It turned out that those young men did not have to go."[1]

"Some anthropologists thought that the spiritual leaders were always men," I told her. I wondered just how she'd answer.

Daisy shook her head, the beginning of a smile tipping her mouth. "That is not true. There's a lot anthropologists don't know and will never know."

My family and I had not visited the Fort Hall Reservation much. Several mixed bands of Shoshone and Bannock were placed there in the 1860s, and after 1907, the government moved the Lemhi Shoshone from Salmon, Idaho, to Fort Hall. I had few contacts or friends there. It was a unique honor to be invited to visit this special Sun Dance. Instead of being held in a very public place, as is the Sun Dance at Wind River, this one was tucked away in a remote part of the Fort Hall Reservation. The written directions to the Sun Dance were intentionally vague. I was told not to worry, the way would be marked.

The way *was* marked but not with written signs. There were bundles of sticks bound together at each turning point. Sometimes there was a strip of red cloth. My family and I thought it was like going on a treasure hunt. I thought at the time that these markers were another indication that the Sun Dance leaders did not encourage casual spectators, only those with a special need to attend a Sun Dance. Highway turned to blue gravel turned to red dirt turned to sand turned to cattle wallows. The area was remote, near Bannock Peak, and the only thing that got us there was that I didn't stop. If I had, we would have been stuck in the sandy loam. But just as the healing ceremony and blessings began, our Jeep lurched into the parking area. Whistles, singing, and the beat of the Sun Dance drums floated on the air.

We followed the music, walking past cars and pickups from Utah, from Wind River, from the Comanche nation in Oklahoma, from the Crow in Montana. We walked past tents where people were sitting around. The Sun Dance lodge was a short distance beyond. About half of the participants in the lodge were women. A woman Sun Dance chief, maybe in her 50s, stood in the middle of the lodge. She wore a traditional squaw dress, maroon and quite plain. I had heard of her; she had quite a strong reputation as a Sun Dance chief. Another chief, a man, was with her and wore a buffalo headdress. Half of his face had been painted black and the other half yellow. The healing ceremonial brushing with eagle feather fans had begun.

Back home in Wisconsin, I did a little digging. The tradition of participation by women comes from the Comanche, who were part of the larger Shoshone nation until about 1800. Shoshone say with some amusement that the Comanche speak Shoshone with a southern drawl. To this day, there is a lot of visiting and intermarriage between the two tribes. There had been Comanche at the Fort Hall Sun Dance and I had seen and spoken with Comanche at Wind River.

As far back as the coming of the horse, the Comanche held ceremonies similar to the Sun Dance. There are stories of a prophetess who directed the construction of a sacred sun lodge.[2] It seems quite likely that this was not an isolated event and that the tradition of women as spiritual equals to men was present in other Shoshone groups, too, and was very old.[3]

Mounted on horses obtained from the Spanish in the late 1600s, Shoshone bands used to range into Saskatchewan, while other bands pushed south into Texas and became the Comanche. Horses allowed them to extend their territory. There were thousands of Shoshone and Comanche in those days, and they were different bands of the same people. Other tribes entered the Plains from both the prairies to the east and the mountains to the west to hunt the vast herds of buffalo. They all now had horses.

Conflict over hunting territory increased. Access to firearms from Hudson's Bay traders in Canada and the French in Louisiana added to the potential for warfare. At the same time, European diseases such as smallpox spread rapidly through the Plains, decimating the tribes.

At times of crisis, new religious movements often appear. The Sun Dance promised healing and power. By the late 18th century, it had become widespread among most of the tribes on the Plains.

A Comanche, Ohamagwaya, also called Yellow Hand[4] after the chiefly color yellow, joined the Eastern Shoshone around 1800. His father had been the great Comanche chief Ecueracapa (Leather Cape), who made a treaty with the Spanish in Santa Fe in 1786.[5] To this day, many Shoshone remember Ohamagwaya as a great chief and medicine man, and attribute the bringing of the Sun Dance to him. If we were to equate a figure from mainstream American culture to Ohamagwaya, it would be someone like Martin Luther King Jr., a charismatic leader who combined religious and political leadership. As a diplomat, Ohamagwaya was the forerunner of Chief Washakie, who must have known him.

There are many recorded recollections of Ohamagwaya. Quinten Quay, a respected Shoshone elder who died in the 1940s, remembered that

> the first man to dance the Sun Dance was Ohamagwaya. A buffalo bull told him to have it. Then an old white-haired man came to him and told him the same. From then on it has been continued. He painted the first Sun Dance doll.[6]

The buffalo is a sacred animal capable of conveying the power of the spiritual world to a mortal. The old white-haired man is not to be disdained as an elder who is weak and tired and has lost his mind. This is a powerful, supernaturally endowed figure that came to transfer power to Ohamagwaya.

The idea of the transfer of prophetic power is an important one. A Sun Dance chief cannot obtain power by himself. He has to be given the power from a supernatural authority. The motivation cannot be selfish; it has to come from outside himself. The chief does not choose himself; rather, he is chosen. To put this in a Judeo-Christian context, the Hebrew prophets were chosen by God; they revealed the unusual power that came from God. Jesus did not choose himself. Jesus was the son of God and descended from a royal lineage, the House of David. Scripture foretold Jesus' prophetic power. True leadership of a religious nature is selfless, not self-appointed. The religious leader is merely a vessel for renewing the society. When the Shoshone pray to Dam Apë in the Sun Dance, they address that power.

"The main Sun Dance originated here long ago," a descendant of Ohamagwaya, John McAdams, recalled.

> My great-grandfather Ohamagwaya said: "I am going to look for *boh* (power)." He had a buffalo robe and he painted this gray with white clay. Then in the evening he went to a butte near Rawlins and slept there overnight. There were no pictographs there but a man came from heaven and told him: "you are looking for great power. I'll tell you what to do. Get a center-forked cottonwood tree and twelve poles; build them like a tipi. Get willows and lean them against the poles. The center pole will represent God; the twelve posts, God's friends. Get a two-year-old buffalo; face it west. Get an eagle; face it east. If anyone sick goes in, the buffalo will help him with good power from the Sun. So will the eagle. Keep the buffalo's hide in shape with a bundle of willows. The cross-sticks will represent the Cross. The first time we're going to dance only five men will dance."[7]

There have been many who have looked for power. This does not mean that all who look receive. Power usually comes through a dream. There is a Shoshone tradition of sleeping near pictographs, which are rock paintings, or petroglyphs, rock carvings. They were made by ancient medicine men and signal a place filled with supernatural power. The motivation to become a religious leader comes in the instructions received in the dream from a supernatural being. The being could be a buffalo or an old man or an eagle or it could be something else.

A somewhat different story of how Ohamagwaya received his power is told by James Trosper, a contemporary Shoshone medicine man and Sun Dance leader, regent of the University of Wyoming, descendant of Ohamagwaya and Washakie, and great-grandnephew of Johnny Trehero, the Sun Dance chief who brought the Sun Dance to the Crow. The producer of a television documentary about Chief Washakie had given me James' name. It wasn't long into our phone conversation that we discovered a shared interest in family history.

But it wasn't until several years later on a summer afternoon in 2005 that we met in person. We sat in the shade of a cottonwood tree, the air still and hot.

"I hear you've been a Sun Dance chief in recent years," I said.

James reached above his head and swatted at the lowest branch of the tree.

> An eagle swooped close to my car at the summit of South Pass. The eagle swooped down again. On a different drive, near Muddy Gap, I'd pulled my car off the road. I heard a growl. It was a wolf. I remembered being told that you should never run away if a wild animal approaches. The wolf kept growling and walked around me but didn't bother me. At last, the wolf simply walked away.

James took a swallow of lemonade and nodded in thought.

> The inspiration for the Sun Dance came to Ohamagwaya from a buffalo that appeared to him at Dinwoody Canyon. Seven arrows were given to him by the *ninimbe*, the little people. The ninimbe gave instructions on how the Sun Dance doll was to be made. They said the doll should be passed down to Ohamagwaya's son Bazil and to his grandson Johnny Trehero."[8]

The Sun Dance doll seems to symbolize the presence of the supernatural vision in the Sun Dance. It is also a tangible symbol of the transfer of power from one Sun Dance chief to another. It is not a doll in the sense of a plaything but is a small humanlike figure, sometimes carved of wood and hung in the Sun Dance lodge during the ceremony.

James says he has Ohamagwaya's Sun Dance doll. He received it from his great-great-uncle Johnny Trehero. Johnny had the doll from his uncle Andrew Bazil, James told me. A dream directed James to visit Tom Yellowtail, the younger brother of Johnny Trehero's longtime assistant. James found Yellowtail on the Crow reservation in Montana. James didn't want to accept the Sun Dance doll but eventually did when Yellowtail, weak and dying, revealed the importance of the doll finding its rightful owner. It was Yellowtail's way of repaying Johnny for having brought the Sun Dance to the Crow, he said. The rightful owner had to be a descendant of both Johnny and Ohamagwaya.

Not everyone at Wind River agrees with James Trosper's version of how he obtained the Sun Dance doll. Shoshone traditions allow that a vision is a source of power and that power does not have to be passed down. But transfer of power helps. Some say that Johnny Trehero gave the doll to his adopted daughter who gave it to Charlie Meyer, also a descendant of Ohamagwaya. When Charlie died, the doll was buried with him. That line of power from Ohamagwaya ended with Charlie. People who believe this version do not agree that James Trosper received Johnny Trehero's power.

"Johnny got his power from his grandfather Bazil," James told me. "Bazil got it from Ohamagwaya who was his father."[9]

I was startled by the thought that flashed through my mind. Now I knew who the Wind River Sacajawea really was. If Bazil's father was Ohamagwaya, his mother could not have been the woman with the Lewis and Clark expedition. No one ever said Ohamagwaya had any ties to Sacajawea. But everyone said that Bazil/Pa:si was the son of Ohamagwaya. The Shoshone also said Paraivo was his mother. Since all documents contemporary to the historical Sacagawea point to her death in 1812 and Paraivo died in 1884, they couldn't have been the same woman. Now I knew who was buried at Wind River: it was Paraivo. I remembered that Paraivo meant *Chief Woman* in Comanche. This could only mean she was the equal of Ohamagwaya. The Shoshone had known all along who she was. She wasn't the woman with Lewis and Clark at all. She was Chief Woman, Chief Ohamagwaya's wife!

Clearly, if power is still traced to Ohamagwaya, his authority is still revered. His wife was also a powerful woman. Her name Paraivo (Chief Woman) tells us that, like her husband, she was Comanche. After Ohamagwaya's death around 1840,[10] his wife may have returned for a while to the Comanche but was living among the Eastern Shoshone by the 1850s. She spoke at the Great Treaty of 1868. Finn Burnett, the former boss farmer at the reservation, recalled that Washakie and other chiefs visited her home at the agency and "listened intensely to her conversation for hours."[11] That Washakie and his chiefs listened to Paraivo means she had a status seldom given to women of that era.

At Wind River from the 1870s until her death in 1884, the widowed Paraivo stayed in a tent outside her son Pa:si's log cabin. He took care of her and she was also known as Bazil umbia, Bazil's mother. Bazil's Shoshone name was Pa:si, which means Bald Eagle.[12] Could anyone imagine a more fitting name for a man who was both a Sun Dance leader and a sub-chief of the great Washakie?

Paraivo's other son, Patseese, whom the whites called Bateez or Baptiste, lived several miles away from his mother's tent and saw little of her. The two brothers did not look alike. Pa:si was tall with a lighter complexion, while Patseese was dark and short. Finn Burnett recalled that the sound of the brothers' two names was "so near alike in pronunciation that it was difficult to know of which they spoke."[13] Patseese is a diminutive of Pa:si, suggesting that Patseese was a younger brother, or maybe, since his height is often described as short, the name referred to the fact that he was a smaller person than Pa:si. This is no different from what I remember from days of playing softball on vacant lots in my neighborhood. There were two Toms. One, a couple of years older, was called Big Tom, and me, Little Tommy.

The two brothers' names may have sounded quite alike to some whites but they were very different people. While Pa:si was a recognized and respected leader, Patseese was not a distinctive person in any way, his contemporaries tell us. He did not show any leadership ability and seems to have spent little time interacting with people around Fort Washakie and the Indian Agency. This is only mentioned because after his death, Patseese is transformed into Sacagawea's son Jean-Baptiste Charbonneau by the boosters of the Wind River Sacajawea.

Paraivo died peacefully at Wind River in April 1884. She was very old, although exactly how old is unknown. Both Pa:si and Patseese passed away within two years of the death of Paraivo.

Two decades later, a white woman from the University of Wyoming decided to look for Sacagawea's trace at Wind River. It was just that simple, except—it wasn't that simple. In fact, it was too simple. The logical place to have looked for her would have been in Salmon, Idaho, or Fort Hall where the Lemhi had been moved in 1907. Those were Sacagawea's people.

Even though Grace Hebard wanted Paraivo to be the rediscovered Sacajawea, the old woman was never called Sacajawea or Sacagawea at Wind River during her lifetime. We have many testimonies to this.[14] White officials called her Bazil umbia. Among the Shoshone, she was always known as Paraivo (variously spelled), Comanche for Chief Woman or Peace Chief.[15] A peace chief was distinguished from a war chief and represented family groups. The peace chiefs selected one of their number to lead for the season, with the other peace chiefs continuing to function as advisors.[16]

Grace Hebard did not know that Paraivo really was a Comanche title.[17] She accepted Reverend Roberts' mistranslation of her Shoshone name as Water White Woman. Hebard must have wondered why her Shoshone informants kept translating *Bazil's mother* as *Chief Woman*, a name Hebard added to Roberts' mistranslation.

Hebard provided several other names for the Wind River Sacajawea. These names were not taken from the Shoshone but from unpublished materials written to the Lemhi Shoshone by a former trader, John Rees, who had collected his stories almost 100 years after the Lewis and Clark expedition.[18] According to Rees, Paraivo was also known as Wadzewipe (Lost Woman) and Bohenaive (Grass Woman).[19] Hebard explained that the name Lost Woman was given to Sacajawea by the Comanche after she left them and finally relocated among the Wyoming Shoshone. Hebard cites no source for this idea. There was no reason to bestow a number of names on the Wind River Sacajawea, except that they helped obscure Paraivo's true identity.

The trader John Rees had provided a collective name for three Shoshone girls he says were captured by the Blackfeet and later sold or traded to the Hidatsa—Bohenaive, meaning Maidens of the Grass People. Po-pank, one of the girls, escaped and returned to her Lemhi people. The other two, Penzo-bert and Wadze-wipe, who later became Sacajawea, did not escape. They became the two wives of Toussaint Charbonneau.[20] Strangely, Hebard took the Grass Woman name plus the Lost Woman name, as well as the mistranslation of Paraivo and applied them all to the Wind River Sacajawea. Penzo-bert became Otter Woman, according to Hebard, and was said to be the "other woman," the second wife of Charbonneau, left behind because of her pregnancy. The original journals of the Lewis and Clark expedition mention none of this.

Pa:si and Patseese were brothers. Their parents were Paraivo and Ohamagwaya. Now the pieces of the puzzle fit together!

Paraivo was a woman of accomplishment and with Ohamagwaya brought the Sun Dance to the Shoshone. She spoke at the Great Treaty of 1868. Paraivo was Chief Woman, a recognized diplomat, the wife and ally of the great Ohamagwaya and the mother of another diplomat, sub-chief Pa:si. Chief Washakie held her in high regard. Shoshone oral tradition said all these things.

Grace Hebard stole Paraivo's accomplishments and added them to the accomplishments of the historical Sacagawea. The equation reads: Historical Sacagawea + Paraivo = Wind River Sacajawea.

# Chapter 10

# Graven in Stone

I have a photograph of Mary Birdabove, taken in the early 1900s. She wears a calico dress with elk teeth sewn in a line from one shoulder to the other in the old style. The dress is long, down to the middle of her calves, the hem meeting high moccasins. Mary Birdabove's outfit is typical of its time. Shoshone women were traditionally modest and would not show their legs. When they sat on the ground, they always made certain their ankles were covered.

The 2003 statue of Sacajawea in the Sacajawea Cemetery is not dressed like Mary Birdabove. The statue is barefoot. Sacajawea holds the hem of her mid-calf buckskin dress to wade in the Pacific Ocean. Her lower legs are bare. Bud Boller, the sculptor, is Shoshone, but he didn't want his Sacajawea to necessarily look like a Shoshone woman.[1] Sacajawea's heroic qualities go beyond tribal background and origin, he told me. The statue is not a historic construction of how Sacajawea might have looked. It is a contemporary interpretation of her spirit.

The statue holds a sand dollar, later to be carried back to Wind River and presented to Chief Washakie. The sand dollar not only offers tangible proof that Bazil's mother had indeed been to the Pacific with Lewis and Clark but also symbolizes a transfer of power. With the sand dollar, Sacajawea bestows her experience to Chief Washakie. Now he can negotiate with the white man more successfully. But it was really Paraivo who did all these things. Sacagawea was a teenager when she was with Lewis and Clark. She died young. She had not achieved the status of peace chief or diplomat or Sun Dance chief. To see a woman transfer power to an important chief tells a deeper story about Shoshone tradition: women have supernatural power that could be transferred to men.

The Sacajawea Cemetery attracts more visitors than the Washakie Cemetery. Chief Washakie is only locally notable, even though his statue

stands in the capitol building in Washington, D.C. The historic Sacagawea holds the national imagination because she made the trek with
Lewis and Clark carrying an infant. At Wind River, Sacajawea isn't
merely the mother who carried her baby thousands of miles and secured
the help of her Idaho Shoshone people for the Lewis and Clark expedition. The Wind River Sacajawea is the historical Sacagawea with fictionalized details added by Hebard to keep her alive until 1884, with Paraivo
folded in.

Sacajawea's cemetery is a 40-acre parcel of land surrounded by steel
fence posts and barbed wire. Trees or bushes would never grow because
the cemetery has no irrigation of any kind. Keeping up a restful, park-like
cemetery is a fairly recent American idea. The first park-like cemetery
detached from a church was Mt. Auburn in Boston in the 19th century.

Sacajawea
statue
designed by
Bud Boller,
erected in
2003 in the
Sacajawea
Cemetery,
Wind River
Reservation,
Wyoming.
Photo by
Sara Wiles.

By then, many Americans no longer believed that the dead were part of a specific Christian congregation that would rise from the dead at the second coming of Christ. Indians had no idea of a burial ground like that.

Shoshone used to place the deceased in inaccessible locations in canyons or rock crevasses away from human habitation. Memorialization was never part of their beliefs, nor were birth and death dates. The dead were not to be visited because their spirits stayed around the body. The spirit could call the living to it, especially in a dream. Such a dream might be a warning of impending disaster, even death. Now most Shoshone bury their dead in the Sacajawea Cemetery.

Even today, reminiscing about the dead is to be avoided; where they died is to be avoided; their bodies are to be avoided. I once made the mistake of asking about a friend who had died while I was away from the reservation. This was met with silence. No one wanted to talk about my friend or his funeral. Once the dead are dead, they are traditionally never discussed.

Reverend John Roberts and Grace Hebard corresponded throughout the 1920s and into the 1930s, planning improvements to the mission cemetery. In keeping with the Christian notion of a cemetery housing converts who would be resurrected at the Second Coming, Reverend Roberts wanted to solidify the ties between the Shoshone and the mission. After all, he had baptized and converted most of them. Grace Hebard was interested in promoting the final burial place and memory of Sacajawea by renaming the cemetery and erecting monuments to her memory.

Roberts and Hebard decided the name was to be changed to Sacajawea Cemetery. A wooden stile to access the cemetery from the road, a granite stone wall to enclose the entire 40 acres, iron gates, stone steps, a marble bench at the foot of Sacajawea's grave from which to look out over the plains to the east and imagine the Shoshone as they once were— riding horses and hunting buffalo—those were some of their ideas to enhance the cemetery.[2] Most of these never happened.

August 1931 saw a ceremony honoring Sacajawea. Dick Washakie, son of the old chief, placed a bronze plate at Paraivo's resting place.[3] Two years later on Memorial Day, a more impressive ceremony took place. Gravestones for Bazil and Baptiste, chiseled from local Lander granite, were set in concrete on either side of the bronze plaque to Sacajawea. Grace Hebard had ordered and paid for the stones, an act that received much newspaper publicity, right down to revealing the cost of $75 for each.[4]

The larger gravestone is for the "papoose of the Lewis and Clark Expedition," as it reads on the monument, with the corresponding birth date of February 11, 1805. "Died on this reservation 1885," the stone records. "Buried west in the Wind River Mountains AD 1933." The last date refers to the erection of the monument itself, not Patseese's burial in the mountains. For both monuments, the granite is rough-hewn except for the polished stone face containing the lettering. The lettering is poorly executed—uneven spacing, shallow engraving—and the monuments themselves are not set in a base. They are simply slabs stuck into concrete and have obviously recently been reset, or the concrete foundation has been repaired.

Grace Hebard also bought a monument for Barbara Baptiste Meyers, a granddaughter of the Wind River Sacajawea. That stone is somewhat smaller than that of her father and uncle and proclaims her relationship to Sacajawea.

There is no evidence that any Shoshone asked for these gravestones or wanted them erected. For many years they were the only granite monuments in the cemetery. More than anything else, the stones put up for Sacajawea and her family represent the imposition of the culture of the dominant society on the Shoshone.

The 1933 service of dedication of these stones included the singing of two hymns by Shoshone girls and an address by Reverend Roberts' successor at the mission church. His address expressed appreciation to Grace Hebard and was simultaneously interpreted into Shoshone by Lynn St. Clair.[5] Reverend Roberts also spoke, thanking the American Legion post in Lander for assistance in the commemoration of the graves of 36 Shoshone soldiers and scouts who had served with the United States during the mop-up of the Plains tribes in the 1870s. He showed gratitude to the great crowd of, as the Lander paper put it, "white people who with the Indians felt a common reverence for the dead and appreciation of the sacrifices they made."[6]

During his last years, Chief Washakie initiated a meal of crackers, raisins, cheese, and an orange at the annual Memorial Day ceremonies at the cemetery. It was always served in a paper bag so the Shoshone could take it home.[7] It was a mini-give-away/funeral feast to commemorate all the deceased rather than one individual. We don't know how many Shoshone actually came into the cemetery to get food.

This same meal was distributed to everyone at the 1933 ceremony. It was a way of tying the memory of the chief to Sacajawea. Washakie had died only 33 years before and his son was now considered chief. Only the very oldest Shoshone had known Paraivo, and they were young when she was very old. But because Paraivo had been transformed into Sacajawea in just the past 30 years, her presence and importance was now equal to or even surpassed that of Washakie.

The annual Memorial Day service had a different special feature each year. In 1935, for example, there was a reenactment of the burial of the Wind River Sacajawea.[8] In 1941, a thousand people attended the unveiling

Lynn St. Clair as Reverend John Roberts in a Sacajawea Pageant in 1935 at the Shoshone Indian School.

of a large granite boulder with a bronze plaque put up by the Historical Landmark Commission of the State of Wyoming.[9] It still stands by the side of Highway 287, a major route to the Tetons and Yellowstone, pointing west to the Sacajawea Cemetery. The governor spoke at the dedication, so did the mayor of Lander. Chief Dick Washakie and his son Marshall took part in the dedication, again linking old Chief Washakie and Sacajawea.[10]

Not all attempts to memorialize Sacajawea at Wind River met with success. An appropriation for a large memorial at the Sacajawea Cemetery died in the United States Senate in 1936. It wasn't the right moment; controversy about when and where the historical Sacagawea had actually died still raged. South Dakota claimed her; so did North Dakota and Wyoming. Yet almost 30 years later, in 1963, the Daughters of the American Revolution reinforced that the woman with the Lewis and Clark expedition had died at Wind River.[11] The organization dedicated a six-foot high rough-hewn granite monument to be erected in the cemetery. The three daughters of Reverend Roberts were in attendance. Seated with the speakers were a grandson and a great-grandson of the Wind River Sacajawea. Only a handful of Landerites attended the event. The governor and a former senator were expected to attend but did not show. By this time, of course, Clark's 1825–28 cashbook had come to light with its notation of when Sacagawea had died.

By 1973, the Daughters of the American Revolution had a problem on their hands. The Malheur Chapter of the DAR dedicated a headstone at the grave of Jean-Baptiste Charbonneau in Danner, Oregon.[12] But if he died there—and newspaper accounts of his death in 1866 say this is so—the DAR monument to Sacajawea at Wind River is a mistake. The National DAR did not answer my written request for an explanation.

In 2000 Jean-Baptiste Charbonneau's gravesite in Oregon was rededicated. More than 300 people attended, including representatives from the Lemhi Shoshone and the Hidatsa. The Eastern Shoshone of Wind River were not in any way involved in the commemoration. The Western Shoshone now maintain the site, only because this is their aboriginal territory.[13]

For a number of years, the Lemhi Shoshone have been re-establishing their connection with Sacajawea (which they spell with a *j* and believe is a

Inscription on the Sacajawea monument at the Sacajawea Cemetery, Wind River Reservation, Wyoming. Photo by Sara Wiles.

Shoshone name, not Hidatsa). They are looking for a burial ground near the site of Fort Manuel Lisa in South Dakota in the hopes of finding some evidence of where Sacagawea lies. They're not interested in exhuming the body but in commemorating her memory. The Lemhi and the city of Salmon, Idaho, have joined together to develop a 71-acre interpretive park in Salmon to celebrate the life and culture of Sacajawea and the Lemhi people.

The Lemhi idea of celebrating life with the continuity of their culture contrasts starkly with the commemoration of the death of Sacajawea at Wind River by the white authorities. It is an important difference, between using the life and heritage of Sacagawea to create a new and improved sense of Lemhi identity and focusing on Sacajawea's death and final resting place, thereby seeing Shoshone culture and people as a thing of the past.

Ironically, Paraivo's body may not even be in the Sacajawea Cemetery. Reverend Roberts' parish records indicate burial, but the plaque by the Boller statue at the crest of the hill tells a different story: "The Eastern Shoshones believe Sacajawea is buried in the Wind River Mountains west of here." Family tradition has it that Bazil's mother's body was moved from the cemetery after Roberts had officiated at her burial.[14] Translation: the Shoshone were in control all the time. Regardless of what the whites tried to impose on them, the most sacred Shoshone beliefs remained intact.

# Chapter 11

# Honoring Sacajawea?

Jarod walked across the room to his father's desk. "I'm going to show you what the government just did to us," he said. "Remember the first Sacajawea stamp?"

I actually did remember it. At the time of the 150th anniversary of the Lewis and Clark expedition in 1954, I was an 11 year-old stamp collector. Every commemorative that came along, I collected it.

I nodded. "Sure. I think I even have one at home in my old stamp album. It was a 3-cent first-class stamp with Sacajawea standing in front of a canoe, right? She was slightly behind Lewis and Clark. She was pointing the way."

"That's the one. They put the dates 1804 for the expedition and 1954 for the 150th at the top of the stamp," Jarod said. He was rummaging through a desk drawer, searching for something.

I waited and looked around the room. On the wall facing me hung a photo grouping of his family, who just happened to include Chief Washakie, Narkok, and Tigee—all famous Shoshone leaders.

"Okay," he said, pulling up a chair. "Here it is. Check this out."

Jarod had a clear plastic sleeve with a first edition of the new "Legends of the West" stamp series, issued in 1994. Sacagawea—spelled Hidatsa-style with a *g*—was one of three women; Annie Oakley and Nellie Cashman were the others. Sacagawea was in three-quarters face, as if looking down the trail, a cradleboard on her back.

Jarod pointed at her. "Not even Shoshone beadwork."

It was true. The woman of the stamp wore a buckskin dress with Plains geometric beadwork, not the traditional Shoshone rose.

"No dates," Jarod winced. "Her death date isn't there."

By this time, I had become pretty well convinced that Sacagawea did not live until 1884. I didn't know how to reply to Jarod. I didn't have to say anything. He wanted to talk.

"It's an insult from the government," he said, eyes narrowing. "Look how they spelled her name."

The stamp was one more indication that the white man knows it all.

Jarod put down the plastic sleeve on the coffee table. Restlessly, he rubbed his chin. I wished I could think of something supportive to say. I've known Jarod since he was born. I used to visit with his dad back when I lived with Tom Wesaw.

"There was a committee," he said. "We wrote letters to congressmen about the date and the name. We never got an answer."

The stamp spoke loud and clear, I knew. Once again, the U.S. government had ignored and put down the Eastern Shoshone. The honorable thing to do would have been to answer the tribe's letters.

Jarod's eyes darted around the room. "We know that Sacajawea was at the signing of the Great Treaty," he told me. "My mother noticed that the artist of that stamp didn't even take the time to find out what our beadwork is like. Nothing about the stamp is genuine."

A few years later, more anger surfaced at Wind River. The government had decided to strike a new dollar coin, a major attempt by Congress to honor a woman. It was supposed to be a big improvement over the Susan B. Anthony dollar coin that had been unsuccessful with the American public because it was similar in size and color to a quarter. The new dollar coin would honor Sacagawea. It was to be larger than the Susan B. Anthony and gold in color. Because of its size and color, the Sacagawea dollar would circulate widely, it was hoped.

Once again, the government snubbed the Eastern Shoshone.

The children's book author Kenneth Thomasma filled me in on the controversy. I happened to be in his home town of Jackson Hole, Wyoming. I had read Thomasma's book on Sacagawea, and my daughters loved his books about the lives of Shoshone children. Thomasma knew a lot about the politics behind the stamp and the coin.

"There were people at Wind River who would have liked to have been considered," he said.

"They were angry at the government ignoring them?" my daughter Cleo asked.

He took a sip of coffee. "Um-hmm. It's a darn shame the Wind River people were completely ignored. The model is a Shoshone-Bannock named Randy'L He-dow Teton from the Fort Hall Reservation."

"No lineal connection to the Wind River Sacajawea?" I asked.

Thomasma nodded. "The sculptor for the coin is a woman named Glenna Goodacre. She lives in New Mexico. She asked around in Santa Fe if anyone knew of a Shoshone girl who could model for her. It didn't take Goodacre long to find a model. Nothing against Randy Teton."[1]

The next day, I drove back to Wind River. I happened to bring up the coin to an old friend.

"Oh yeah," she said. "That was Randy Teton, a relative of mine. But she's never lived here and she's not related to Sacajawea. Why they selected her and not somebody from here, I'll never know. Why did Randy agree to pose?"

The Eastern Shoshone had been cut out of the decision of who should model for the coin. Santa Fe is far removed from Shoshone territory. Goodacre had gone to the prestigious American Indian Institute for the Arts to search for her model. She had inquired at the desk. In no time, she had her model. Once again, the Eastern Shoshone felt ignored by the government.

At the gas station on the Wind River reservation, I ran into another friend. I told him I had just heard how the model for the Sacajawea dollar was selected.

"Sure, I know about it," my friend said, pushing the brim of his cowboy hat up with his forefinger. "She's a student at some college in New Mexico. That papoose on the coin wasn't even Randy's baby. What a fake. Why didn't they choose a Wind River woman with her own baby?"

The final insult was that Randy Teton received recognition at the Washington, D.C., ceremony to unveil the coin. Randy Teton is a fine person, people told me. But a lineal descendant could have been at that ceremony. An Eastern Shoshone woman should have been at that ceremony and had her picture taken with Mrs. Clinton, people said.

Several years later, I happened to be talking to a relative of a good Shoshone friend of mine. Her grandfather had told her that she was a lineal descendant of Patseese whom she called Baptiste, as Grace Hebard had. As she talked, she became agitated. "The so-called Shoshone have stolen Sacajawea," she said.

I didn't understand what she meant. "So-called?"

"The Lemhi! These Lemhi are bandwagon people. Not real descendants. They're descended from Cameahwait, her brother. A bunch of bums only out for their own gain."

By now, she was really angry. She mentioned several names of Lemhi who claim that Sacajawea died in South Dakota, not in Wyoming.

It was hot. We were talking in the full afternoon sun. I shifted on my feet.

"My grandfather told me the truth," she said. Her words came hard and from deep within. "No one can say different and still be telling the truth. *We are descended from Baptiste!* Do you know they had a reunion of those Lemhi descendants of Sacajawea's brother Cameahwait?"

She was waiting for me to answer. I said, "I hadn't heard about that."

"They want to glory off someone else's name. A sign of real selfishness." Selfishness is considered one of the worst traits a Shoshone can display.

On the drive back to my motel, I thought about the Lemhi and Wind River people, about how the Sacajawea controversy had pushed them farther and farther apart. Until the 1990s, no one at Wind River ever mentioned the Lemhi. They talked about the Fort Hall people, their relatives, but never singled out the Lemhi.

It's different now. Sacagawea was an Agaidika, a Salmon-eater or Lemhi Shoshone. Because of a short-lived Mormon mission in the 1850s, they came to be called the Lemhi Shoshone. They are going through a period of reclaiming their ties to their homeland near Salmon, Idaho, taken from them by the United States in 1907. They were forced to relocate among the Fort Hall Shoshone near Pocatello, Idaho. In order to reclaim their homeland, the Lemhi have also tried to reclaim their connection to Sacagawea. Recently, they've built a Sacajawea Center in Salmon. It focuses on the Agaidika Shoshone perspective.[2] The Sacajawea Center has the stamp of approval of the city of Salmon, the state of Idaho, and the federal government through the Bureau of Land Management. All of this official recognition goes far beyond that at Wind River. Wind River only has a cemetery named after her, a statue in the cemetery, and a handful of markers. What is being depicted at Wind River is simply an alleged burial place, selected by one white woman.

In the summer of 2006 I happened to talk with an Idaho Shoshone visiting friends at Wind River.

He faced me straight on and looked directly in my eyes. "You're interested in family history? I can tell you something that you ought to know," he volunteered.

I shrugged. I felt uncomfortable. I hadn't asked him anything and his tone was confrontational.

"Sacajawea was a Lemhi and belongs in Idaho," he said. "She's not related to anyone here. She's not buried here. She died in North or South Dakota where she is probably buried. The Shoshone who say she is here at Wind River are all *ishump*." I knew that word very well as I'd heard it before. It means *liar*.

I walked away with an even stronger sense that the Wind River Sacajawea has created more enmity than anything else between Shoshone peoples. Once the idea that Paraivo had really been Sacajawea took root, the plant flourished. But today the soil is very rocky and dry.

The Daughters of the American Revolution are among the caretakers of the Wind River Sacajawea legend today. Their involvement goes back to Grace Hebard's membership in the organization. Besides the major monument to the Wind River Sacajawea the Wyoming Daughters erected in 1963, in October 2006 the Namaqua Chapter of Colorado gave a banner to the Eastern Shoshone Cultural Center. The 6′ × 4′ banner was a backdrop for a presentation called "Sacajawea Reminisces the Expedition

Banner donated by the DAR to the Shoshone Cultural Center, 2006.

of Lewis and Clark" presented to other DAR chapters, civic organizations, schools, and church groups. The bicentennial of the Lewis and Clark expedition has come and gone. The banner—which they call a mural—is of no further use to the DAR and so they have now donated it to the Eastern Shoshone Cultural Center.[3]

On the left-hand side of the mural stand Clark's slave York, Meriwether Lewis, William Clark, Lewis' dog, and finally Sacagawea with the infant Jean-Baptiste on her back. Sacagawea points to the Missouri River with her left hand and to the stick drawings of a map in the dirt with her right. The slave York and Sacagawea stand on either side of Lewis and Clark. In reality, they would never have had such a prominent position. A slave and an Indian woman attached to a white man were only property in 1805.

It's the Hidatsa chief Sheheke and Sacagawea who are pointing the way up the Missouri to the white men, but the theme is false. As a captive from an enemy tribe, Sacagawea would not have been worthy to stand next to Chief Sheheke. Sacagawea was not a guide, beyond recognizing certain landmarks from her childhood. Her role was two-fold: interpreter to the Shoshone people and go-between with the tribes. The idea of Sacagawea as a guide comes from the novelist Eva Emery Dye. It is fiction.

The banner was dedicated at the Cultural Center with a traditional feast of buffalo stew and fry bread. Seventy Shoshone welcomed the

Daughters and their banner. Shoshone children in traditional costume danced to drums and singing. Descendants of the Wind River Sacajawea came forward to speak about her and read a long list of names of her descendants. Hebard's fabricated Wind River Sacajawea had completely displaced Paraivo.

A Daughter wrote of the experience that "it was moving to hear those names read, rather as a tribute to America's most famous heroine!"[4] Two hundred years after the end of the Lewis and Clark expedition, the DAR is still white-washing Sacagawea's life story. The real story is that Sacagawea marks the beginning of Euro-American oppression of the Shoshone. From the time she was sold or gambled to Charbonneau, she was white man's chattel, to be used as he wanted. When the Lewis and Clark expedition contacted her people, the Lemhi, they had already felt the adverse effects of domination by the Blackfeet and their British guns. The Shoshone would dwindle in numbers and their resources decline for another hundred years or more. Over and over again, the white power structure threatened the Wind River reservation and Shoshone economic security. Sacagawea, through no fault of her own, is a harbinger of tragedy.

A completely different image of an Indian woman emerges in what we know of Paraivo. She represents the days when the Shoshone were free. As a peace chief, she, along with her husband and later their son, Pa:si, tried to stem the tide of American expansion. They obtained a fine reservation for the Eastern Shoshone through their skilled diplomacy. As the Sun Dance that they brought to the Shoshone lives on, Paraivo and Ohamagwaya embody the hope of Shoshone pride and self-determination now and in the future.

It's easier for the Lemhi. They never had a Grace Hebard to superimpose a different identity on Paraivo. They never had the Daughters of the American Revolution planting monuments in their graveyard and hanging banners at the Cultural Center. The Lemhi didn't have the weight of a contrived white woman's theory of what happened to Sacagawea on their reservation.

In 2001, the Hunkpapa Sioux asked the Lemhi, not the Eastern Shoshone, to help honor the historical Sacagawea. They went to the old site of Fort Manuel Lisa, which is on the Hunkpapas' reservation. The tribes believe that Sacagawea died there in 1812 and was buried there. Her spirit needed to be respected, the Hunkpapa told the Lemhis.

There's no discernible burial ground at the old site. Much of where Fort Manuel Lisa once stood has flooded over and is covered with the waters of the dammed-up Missouri River. The Hunkpapas joined with the Lemhi to perform a ceremony to calm Sacagawea's restless spirit. Eagles—a propitious sign—appeared in the sky at the right time.[5]

Paraivo's spirit deserves honor, too. Paraivo helped bring the Sun Dance to the Eastern Shoshone. She spoke at the signing of the Great Treaty. Chief Washakie listened to her and respected her. Paraivo—not just her son Pa:si—may well have transferred Sun Dance leadership. She is the ancestor of many well-known Eastern Shoshone who have had a great impact on today's tribe, the ancestor of everybody claiming descent from the fictitious Sacajawea. How many have ever carried the title, Chief Woman?

# The Wind River Sacajawea Who's Who

**Bazil, Andrew**—son of Pa:si, major informant to Grace Hebard and Dr. Eastman. Died 1932.

**Boller, Bud**—a noted sculptor residing in Dubois, Wyoming, where he has a gallery. Member of the Shoshone tribe.

**Brackenridge, James**—lawyer and traveler who went up the Missouri with Sacajawea and Toussaint Charbonneau to Fort Manuel Lisa in 1811.

**Bridger, Jim**—well-known American fur trader who came to the central Rockies in the 1820s. Established a trading post near Green River, Wyoming. One of his wives may have been a daughter of Washakie, who was a firm friend and ally.

**Burnett, Fincelius**—hired as boss farmer—to teach the Shoshone how to farm—at Wind River reservation in 1870s, continued to live in the area. Daughter married into the prominent Simpson family of Wyoming and son married a daughter of Pa:si. Died 1933.

**Charbonneau, Jean-Baptiste**—the papoose son of Sacajawea and Toussaint Charbonneau during the Lewis and Clark expedition. Educated by Captain Clark in St. Louis and Prince Paul in Germany. Career as trapper and guide in the West. Died in 1866 near Danner, Oregon.

**Charbonneau, Lizette**—infant daughter of Sacajawea and Toussaint Charbonneau, born at Fort Manuel Lisa in 1812. Fate unknown.

**Charbonneau, Toussaint**—French-Canadian trader hired at the Mandan villages as an interpreter for the Lewis and Clark expedition, owner of Sacajawea and father of Jean-Baptiste. He took both of them with him on the expedition as it left the Mandan villages in April, 1805. He undoubtedly had other wives and offspring. Date of death unknown; possibly 1843.

**Clark, William**—co-leader of the Lewis and Clark expedition, superintendent of Indian Affairs for the Louisiana Purchase.

**Eastman, Dr. Charles**—Dakota Sioux homeopathic physician whose Sioux name was Ohiyesa. Appointed by Bureau of Indian Affairs to investigate the different stories about what happened to Sacajawea, 1924–25. He allowed the exhumation of the body of Pa:si (Bazil), said to be Sacajawea's son, in order to find a Jefferson medal, in 1925.

**Hebard, Grace**—Professor of Political Economy at the University of Wyoming and author of the Wind River Sacajawea theory. Born 1861, died 1936.

**Irwin, Dr. James**—U.S. Indian Service agent at Wind River, 1870s and again in the early 1880s. His wife Sarah said to have taken down Paraivo's stories, which allegedly were destroyed in a fire.

**Lewis, Meriwether**—co-leader of the Lewis and Clark expedition.

**Ohamagwaya**—Son of Comanche Chief Ecueracapa. Later, chief himself of the Wyoming Shoshone. Famous medicine man. Name means Yellow (Back of) Hand; yellow is a chief's color. Thought to have been born about 1765 and died about 1840.

**Otter Woman**—the name given by Grace Hebard to the second wife of Charbonneau, claiming that it was Otter Woman who died at Fort Manuel Lisa, not Sacajawea.

**Paparosa**—a female shaman. Had a vision, sponsored a Sun Dance, and continued the tradition of including women as shamans and sun dancers.

**Paraivo**—Comanche woman whose name means Chief Woman. Co-bringer of the Sun Dance to the Eastern Shoshone, wife of Ohamagwaya and mother of Pa:si and Patseese. Identified twenty years after her death in 1884 as Sacajawea.

**Pa:si**—Anglicized name Bazil. Son of Paraivo and Ohamagwaya, brother of Patseese, and father of Andrew Bazil. Name means Bald Eagle, indicating honor and power as a medicine man. Leader of a small band of Comanche and other Indians, one of Washakie's most trusted subchiefs. Took care of his mother in her old age.

**Patseese**—Anglicized name Bateez or Baptiste. Son of Paraivo and Ohamagwaya, brother of Pa:si. Name means "Little Pa:si" or "Little Bald Eagle." No formal education. Illiterate and no notable leadership qualities. Lived some distance from his mother in her old age. Said to have been Jean-Baptiste Charbonneau by Grace Hebard.

**Patten, James**—lay teacher and preacher at Wind River, 1870s, friend of Dr. Irwin, and acting agent 1877–1880. Later, pharmacist and real estate speculator off the reservation. Died 1927.

**Rees, John**—born 1868. Came to the Salmon, Idaho, area in 1877 and became a trader with the Lemhi and informant for Elliott Coues. Editor of the last rendition of the Biddle edition of the Journals of Lewis and Clark, 1893.

**Roberts, Reverend John**—Episcopal missionary to Wind River Shoshone 1883–1949.

**Sacagawea**—Lemhi Shoshone from Idaho or Montana, accompanied Lewis and Clark expedition with spouse Toussaint Charbonneau and infant son Jean-Baptiste. Linguists have concluded the name is not Shoshone and does not mean Boat-Pusher or Canoe-Launcher. Her name is Hidatsa and should be spelled either Sacagawea or Sakakawea. It means Bird Woman. She was sometimes referred to as Bird Woman by Clark, further proof that her name was Hidatsa. *Sacajawea* is a spelling fixed by the Biddle edition of the Lewis and Clark Journals and by Grace Hebard.

**Schroer, Blanche Moore**—daughter of Wind River reservation physician. Outspoken opponent of the Wind River Sacajawea theory.

**Shoshone, Eastern**—Eastern-most group of Shoshone Indians, residing mostly in Wyoming and settled on Wind River reservation in 1871.

**Shoshone, Lemhi**—Sacajawea's people. Also known as the Northern Shoshone, their first reservation was near Salmon, Idaho. They lost their reservation in 1907 and were incorporated with Fort Hall Shoshone—Bannock. Trying to recover their lost land and heritage.

**Washakie**—chief of the Eastern Shoshone from the 1840s until his death in 1900, famous for negotiating skills and leadership.

**Wesaw, Tom**—native healer and Sun Dance chief who came from a family of religious leaders and healers. He led Sun Dances from the 1930s until 1966. He died a few years later at the age of 87.

# Appendix B

# Sacagawea + Paraivo = The Fictitious Wind River Sacajawea

I. Similarities

The three life stories have only two elements in common: each traveled with whites and each saw a big fish. Even these two similarities have differences:

**Table I**

|  | Paraivo | The historical Sacagawea | The Wind River Sacajawea |
|---|---|---|---|
| **Traveled with Whites** | Was with first *ava-je-mear* or "those who went by long ago." That could be any number of white traders or trappers. | Traveled with the Lewis and Clark expedition as interpreter and mediator with her Shoshone people, particularly in the procurement of horses. | Traveled with the Lewis and Clark expedition as guide, pilot, and interpreter. |
| **Saw a Big Fish** | The beached whale was intact. Paraivo hacked off blubber. | Only the whale's skeletal remains were to be seen. All blubber had been removed by local Indians. | Same as Paraivo. |

94

II. Differences

Most of the Fictitious Wind River Sacajawea is composed of elements from Paraivo.

## Table 2

| Paraivo | The Fictitious Wind River Sacajawea |
| --- | --- |
| Mother of Pa:si | Adopted mother of Pa:si |
| Came to Wind River from Comanche | Yes |
| Sun Dance Chief | Yes |
| Spoke at Great Treaty, 1868 | Yes |
| Advised Chief Washakie | Yes |
| Died at Wind River, age about 100 | Yes |

And some elements from Sacagawea:

## Table 3

| Sacagawea | The Fictitious Wind River Sacajawea |
| --- | --- |
| Mother of Jean-Baptiste | Mother of Patseese, anglicized to Bateez, further frenchified to Baptiste by Grace Hebard |
| Lemhi Shoshone | Yes |
| Kidnapped as a girl by Hidatsa, traded or gambled to Toussaint Charbonneau | Yes |
| In St. Louis, 1809 | Yes |

III. Unique to the Fictitious Wind River Sacajawea

- Leaves Charbonneau because he mistreats her and also favors another wife, Eagle.
- After wandering, joins Comanche and marries a Comanche named Jerk Meat.
- Has five children with Jerk Meat. When he is killed, she deserts Comanche.
- Goes to Wind River to rejoin Pa:si and Patseese, about 1843.
- Carries a sand dollar on all her journeys. She gives the sand dollar to Chief Washakie. He has it made into a neckerchief holder.

# Appendix C

# The Elements of a Myth

|  | Paraivo | Sacagawea | Wind River Sacajawea |
|---|---|---|---|
| **Name** | Comanche, meaning *Peace Chief.* Spelled *Porivo* by Grace Hebard who was told it meant *Chief* but added John Rees' translation, *Water White Person* (*pa* + *taivo* in Shoshone). Never called Sacajawea at Wind River. Only known as *Paraivo* and *Pa:si umbia* (Bazil's Mother) at Wind River. | Hidatsa, meaning *Bird Woman.* Pronounced Sakakawea (often spelled Sacagawea). The *j* came in through two early editions of the *History of the Lewis and Clark Expedition*—the Biddle edition (1814) and the Coues edition (1893). Her original Shoshone name is unknown. Also called *Janey* by whites. | Shoshone, meaning *Boat Pusher* (according to Rev. John Roberts) or *Travel, with Boats Being Pulled—* Saca-tzaw-meah— (according to John Rees). Also called *Porivo* (Water White Person and Chief Woman) by Rees and Hebard. Also called *Wadze-wipe* (Lost Woman) and *Bohenaive* (Grass Woman) by Hebard. |
| **Tribal Origin** | Comanche. Joined Eastern Shoshone long before the Great Treaty of 1868, along with husband Ohamagwaya. | Lemhi Shoshone from Idaho/Montana. Captured as a girl by Hidatsa. Sold or traded to the French Canadian Toussaint Charbonneau. | Same as Sacagawea. |

(continued)

| | Paraivo | Sacagawea | Wind River Sacajawea |
|---|---|---|---|
| **Culture Change** | Spoke Comanche, Shoshone, some French, some English. | Dressed and acted like a white woman in St. Louis and on trips up and down the Missouri River. | Did not dress and act as a white woman. Spoke Shoshone, maybe Comanche, some French, some English. |
| **Husband(s)** | Ohamagwaya | Toussaint Charbonneau | Toussaint Charbonneau and Jerk Meat |
| **Husband's Other Wives** | Unknown | One other wife (name unknown), left in Mandan villages | Otter Woman, Eagle, possibly also a Ute wife |
| **Biological Children** | Pa:si and Patseese | Jean-Baptiste and Lizette Charbonneau | Jean-Baptiste Charbonneau |
| **Adopted Children** | None | None | Bazil, son of her late sister |
| **Traveled with Whites** | Yes. Was with first *ava-je-mear* or "those who went by long ago." That could be any number of people, white or Indian. | Yes. Went with Lewis and Clark expedition as interpreter and mediator with her Shoshone people. | Yes. Went with Lewis and Clark expedition, functioning as guide, pilot, and interpreter. |
| **Met Her Relatives in Lemhi Country** | No. She was Comanche. She probably never entered Lemhi country in northern Idaho. | Yes. Met her brother Cameawait, chief of the Lemhis. | Same as Sacagawea, plus adopted her late sister's son. |
| **Saw a Big Fish** | Yes, but the beached whale was intact. Paraivo hacked off blubber. | Yes, but only the whale's skeletal remains were to be seen. All blubber had been removed by local Indians. | Same as Paraivo. |
| **Carried a Shell from the Pacific to Wyoming** | No | No | Said to have given a sand dollar to Chief Washakie. He had it made into a neckerchief holder. |

*(continued)*

*(continued)*

|  | Paraivo | Sacagawea | Wind River Sacajawea |
|---|---|---|---|
| **St. Louis** | No connection. May have gone to Comanche country for a period after her husband's death, about 1840. In Wyoming in 1860s with her son, Pa:si. | Came down to St. Louis in 1809 and left Jean-Baptiste to be educated by Clark. Returned to Upper Missouri in 1811. | Came down to St. Louis in 1809, remained for an indeterminate period, probably years. Deserted by Charbonneau for another woman, Eagle. Wandered for many years, settling among the Comanche where she married Jerk Meat and had several children. Left for Wind River about 1843, even though she was not Eastern Shoshone. |
| **Death** | April 1884, Wind River, Wyoming. Said to be 100. | December 1812, Fort Manuel Lisa in South Dakota. Age about 25. | Same as Paraivo. |

# Notes

## 2
## Mistaken Identity

[1] Two spellings—Sacagawea and Sacajawea—appear in the book. The spelling discrepancy is intentional and its importance will reveal itself in the early pages of this book.

[2] The DAR, the Daughters of the American Revolution, is a national organization of women descended from people who participated in the American Revolutionary War. It has local chapters and state organizations and a national headquarters in Washington, DC.

[3] Harold P. Howard, *Sacajawea* (Norman: University of Oklahoma Press, 1971), pp. 189–190.

## 3
## How One Family Became Another

[1] Irving W. Anderson, "J. B. Charbonneau, Son of Sacajawea," *Oregon Historical Quarterly* 71, no. 3 (September 1970): 247–264. See also his "Probing the Riddle of the Bird Woman," *Montana the Magazine of Western History* 23 (1973). The evidence of his death is in the form of a newspaper notice on May 16, 1866, at a stagecoach stop, Inskip Station, near Danner, Oregon. Danner is now a ghost town. He died at the age of 61.

[2] Prof. Slosson and his wife remained good friends of Grace Hebard during her lifetime. Cf. Wenzel, *op. cit.*

[3] Donna J. Kessler. *The Making of Sacajawea—A Euro-American Legend.* Tuscaloosa: The University of Alabama Press, 1996.

[4] Grace R. Hebard. "Pilot of First White Men to Cross the American Continent." *The Journal of American History* 1, no. 3 (1907): 467–484.

[5] H. E. Wadsworth to Rev. John Roberts, Dec. 29, 1941. Roberts files, AHC, Laramie, WY.

[6] *Ibid.* Wadsworth succeeded to the position of agent in 1904, replacing Herman Nickerson. Both men were heavily involved in real estate. Washakie died in 1900 but Wadsworth said that when he came to the Lander area in the spring of 1884, "barely 20 years of age, everything pertaining to the Indians was especially interesting to me. I often visited the Shoshone Agency and Fort Washakie and delighted in talking with the older

members of both tribes—Shoshone and Arapaho. Among them was the outstanding character of old Chief Washakie with whom I became more or less acquainted."

7 Mike Mackey, *Inventing History in the American West: The Romance and Myths of Grace Raymond Hebard*, Powell, WY: Western History Publications, 2005.

8 James Irwin, Agent. *Report to the Commissioner of Indian Affairs for 1876*, pp. 556–557. In his report, Irwin says "the numbers (of Shoshone) must have diminished greatly since Lewis and Clark."

9 Sanderson M. Martin, Agent. *Report to the Secretary of the Interior, House Executive Documents*, 1884.

10 James Patten to Grace Hebard, May 31, 1905. Hebard files, AHC, Laramie, WY. Hebard also lists "a-va-je-mear" as one of several names given to Sacajawea (Hebard, 1932, p. 292).

11 Grace R. Hebard, *Washakie* (Lincoln: University of Nebraska Press, 1995), p. 31. This book was originally published by the Arthur H. Clark Company in 1930.

12 James I. Patten to Grace R. Hebard, May 31, 1906. Hebard files, AHC, Laramie, WY.

13 Dale L. Morgan, ed. "Washakie and the Shoshone" Parts I, II, III, IV. *Annals of Wyoming*, Vols. 24: 140–189; 26: 65–80; 27: 61–81, 198–200; 28: 80–93, 193–207; 29: 86–102, 195–227; 30: 53–89, 1953–1958.

14 Grace R. Hebard. *Sacajawea: Guide and Interpreter of Lewis and Clark.* (Glendale, CA: The Arthur H. Clark Company, 1932), p. 187.

15 Virginia C. Trenholm and Maurine Carley. *The Shoshonis: Sentinels of the Rockies* (Norman: University of Oklahoma Press, 1964).

16 Mary Lou Pence, "Ellen Hereford Washakie of the Shoshones." *Annals of Wyoming* 22, No. 2 (1950): 3–11. Pence says nothing about Ellen Hereford (1878–1950) ever recalling a woman who was known as Sacajawea with Lewis and Clark. Ellen, daughter (or stepdaughter—cf. Ann Hafen, *The Mountain Men and the Fur Trade of the Far West* 7: 247–254) of Lucille Robertson and Robert Hereford, a Virginian was "christened Ellen Lewis, believing that his (Hereford's) wife's genealogy was traceable to Captain Lewis" (p. 5). Her father's ancestry was traceable to the Lees, George Washington, and the present Queen Elizabeth. Ellen married John McAdams (a grandson of Bazil or Pa:si and great-grandson of Paraivo and Ohamagwaya), and the couple had three children: Lonjo (Lonnie), Iva (Norman) and William. Iva died in a tragic family slaying. Ellen divorced McAdams in 1912. She married Charles Washakie in 1917, and Ellen and Charles raised Lydia and her sister Bertha. Her father Robert was a farm and land agent for the Shoshone tribe. A sister of Ellen, Virginia Martinez, born in 1862, is cited by Schroer as testifying that her mother, Lucille, had been around Paraivo on a daily basis, as they lived close to each other on Henry's Fork, and the old woman never said anything about being with Lewis and Clark (cf. Blanche Schroer, "Sacajawea—the Legend and the Truth," *In Wyoming*, Dec.–Jan., 1978). Schroer notes the difference between her information and that recorded by Ellen and Virginia's mother, Lucille, (cf. Hebard, *Sacajawea*, pp. 248–249). Here, Grandma Hereford (Lucille), age about 100 says she "personally knew Porivo ('Chief') well," and that she had traveled with a group of army officers who had become very hungry and ate horses and even dogs (p. 249). She believed that "Porivo" was Sacajawea because "she told of many experiences she had encountered in her past life, otherwise no other person could have told of these experiences unless they had some similar experience. I remember she mentioned something about Clark, but I cannot recall what it was now" (p. 249). The latter statement proves nothing about Paraivo being Sacajawea but suggests that Grandma Hereford had been told the old woman was Sacajawea and altered her story accordingly. A further suggestion that there was bias inserted intentionally into this story is the fact that in Hebard's account, Grandma Hereford's statement is witnessed on Nov. 29, 1926, by James E. Compton,

the translator hired by Hebard for all her 1926 witnessed testimonies, but more impor- tantly, the witnesses listed included one of Grandma Hereford's daughters, Viola Snyder, and her husband, Charles.

17 James I. Patten, Agent. *Shoshone Indian Census,* Nov. 1, 1877. See also William Swagerty, "Marriage and Settlement Patterns of Rocky Mountain Trappers and Traders," *The Western Historical Quarterly* (April 1980): 178. The tribe having the largest number of recorded marriages with trappers was Shoshone, with 16 (p. 165).

18 Mackey, *Inventing History,* p. 67.

19 Susan M. Colby, *Sacagawea's Child* (Spokane: Arthur H. Clark, 2005). See also: Marion Tinling, *Sacajawea's Son* (Missoula, MT: Mountain Press Publishing Co., 2001). Colby's account summarizes the scholarship on Jean-Baptiste Charbonneau. Tinling's book is accurate, written for young readers. Both accounts testify to Jean-Baptiste's death in Oregon in 1866 and discount any connection to Bat-tez or Patseese, whom Hebard called Baptiste, at Wind River.

20 Tinling, *Sacajawea's Son,* pp. 83–104.

21 Anderson, "J. B. Charbonneau."

22 *Ibid.*

23 William Marshall Anderson quoted in Tinling, *Sacajawea's Son,* p. 56.

24 Tinling, *Sacajawea's Son,* p. 68.

25 Hebard, *Sacajawea,* pp. 158–160.

26 Grace Hebard to Mrs. John Campbell, March 29, 1928. Hebard collection, AHC, Laramie, WY.

27 Grace Hebard to Professor William G. Beck, June 19, 1928. Hebard collection, AHC, Laramie, WY.

28 Hebard, *Sacajawea,* p. 179.

29 William Marshall Anderson quoted in Tinling, *Sacajawea's Son,* p. 56.

30 Hebard, *Sacajawea,* pp. 64–67. Hebard admits that the Biddle edition (Coues, ed. 1893) is the only edition that mentions the adoption by Sacajawea of her deceased sister's son while among the Lemhi in 1805. The Shoshone language and kinship terminology use the same term, *bia,* for mother and maternal aunt and those first cousins call each other brother and sister, not cousin. So an adopted child could certainly call his aunt mother and she would call him son. But Hebard cites no awareness of Shoshone kinship termi- nology. The adoption account must be doubted, as the definitive R. G. Thwaites (1904) and G. Moulton (1988) editions of the Journals do not mention it.

31 F. G. Burnett, testimony cited in G. Hebard, *Sacajawea,* p. 230.

32 Fincelius G. Burnett to Grace R. Hebard, February 17, 1930, Hebard files, AHC, Laramie, WY.

33 Hebard, *Sacajawea,* pp. 170–174.

34 *Ibid.*

# 4
# Reservation and Town

1 Joe Kennah's maternal grandfather George Terry was the tribal chairman brutally mur- dered in 1907. Joe's mother, Felicia, was Tom Wesaw's first cousin; their mothers were daughters of John and Julia Enos.

2 Schroer, *Sacajawea,* pp. 21–43.

3 *Ibid.*

# 5
# The Search for Proof You Can See and Touch

[1] Wenzel, *Dr. Grace*, pp. 1–4.

[2] *Ibid.*

[3] *Ibid*

[4] *Ibid.*

[5] *Ibid*

[6] *Ibid.*

[7] *Ibid*

[8] Hebard, *Pilot.*

[9] John C. Luttig, *Journal of a Fur-trading Expedition on the Upper Missouri 1812–1813*, Stella M. Drumm, editor. St. Louis: Missouri Historical Society, 1920.

[10] *Ibid.*, p. 106.

[11] Howard, *Sacajawea*, p. 157.

[12] Richard Edward Oglesby, *Manuel Lisa and the Opening of the Missouri Fur Trade*, pp. 72–73.

[13] Hebard, *Sacajawea*, pp. 111–114.

[14] *Ibid.*

[15] Howard, *Sacajawea*, pp. 141–143.

[16] Colby, *Sacagawea's Child*, p. 72.

[17] Grace Hebard, having no knowledge of the Shoshone language, believed that "Pomp" was a Shoshone name, meaning "head." The Shoshone word for head is "baampi"— close but not exact. Hebard says, without any authority given, that "Pomp is a name meaning head given often to the oldest boy in a Shoshone family, and means 'head' or 'the leader.'" Further "it is bestowed on the eldest son, and thus becomes a title of primogeniture, and the bearer of it is recognized as one having authority" (p. 88). Hebard must have gotten this idea from John Rees' unpublished papers (p. 317). Rees mentions the idea that the name Pomp meant "head" in Shoshone, citing the name of the present chief of the Lemhis "Too-pompy" which means *black-headed* (cf. John E. Rees, *Madame Charbonneau*. Salmon, Idaho: The Lemhi County Historical Society, 1970, p. 9). Most authorities believe the name Pomp, given by Clark to Jean-Baptiste as a toddler, was a nickname that described the antics of the "little dancing boy" that amused Clark and the expedition members and has no connection to the Shoshone word for head.

[18] James Willard Schultz, *Bird Woman: Sacagawea's Own Story*, Boston: Houghton Mifflin, 1918, reprinted by Mountain Meadow Press, 1999, p. 114.

[19] *Ibid.*, p. 133.

[20] Hebard, *Sacajawea*, p. 318. In the bibliography of *Sacajawea*, under the listing of Schultz's book, Hebard wrote: "pure fiction." Hebard may have picked up the name Otter Woman either from Stella Drumm's mention of that name in her edited version of Luttig's Journal or from James Schultz's fictional account, *Bird Woman*. It is also quite likely that Hebard got the information about Otter Woman and the names of the other Shoshone girls captured by the Hidatsa with Sacajawea from John Rees' unpublished materials, as noted above. Rees refers to the captives collectively as "Pooeynaive" (Grass Maidens). Rees, who claimed to know the Shoshone language, goes on to refer to the captives individually as Po Pank (Jumping Fish), Penzobert (Otter Girl?) and Wadziwipe (Lost Woman). These are Rees' spellings. Hebard seems to have borrowed the names Pooenave and Wadziwipe and used them in addition to Porivo as additional names for the Wyoming Sacajawea, as they are inserted in various "testimonies" in her 1932 book. Rees claimed that Wadzewipe was also Sacajawea and says that Po Pank escaped, while Penzobert—Otter Girl's very rough Shoshone equivalent of the Shoshone for otter (pan-

zook)—went with Wadziwipe who later came to be known as Sacajawea. Rees cites no sources for his stories and was not a trained linguist.

Schultz also may have had access to Rees' unpublished materials for his 1918 book, *Bird Woman*. He uses the names Leaping Fish (Po Pank) for one captive girl and Bo I naev (to use Rees' spelling) for Sacajawea, having his fictional chief, Rising Wolf, say "Yes, this was her name, Grass Woman. Later we called her Lost Woman and still later, after the great happening, we named her Water-White-Men or Woman" (cf. Schultz, *Bird Woman*, p. 11). These three names came into Hebard's account as Schultz wrote them, but they probably originated with Rees; it is possible that Schultz, too, knew Rees in the early 1900s; Rees contributed material to the first *Handbook of American Indians* (Frederick W. Hodge, ed., 1907–10, 2 vols.). He also accompanied the editor of the Biddle edition of the Journals of Lewis and Clark, Elliott Coues, in 1893, so was thought to be an early authority on the Shoshone language. Hebard did not acknowledge Rees as the source for her names, attributing their origin to the Shoshone she interviewed. As mentioned above, the only name all the Shoshone seem to have called the old woman was Paraivo, meaning "Chief" or "Chief Woman," not Rees' erroneous translation, "Water-White Man or Woman," which Hebard accepted, adding it to her list of names. Hebard translates Paraivo both as Chief Woman and Water White Woman (or Person) (Rees, *Madame*, pp. 24–25). Obviously, Hebard was told that the name meant Chief or Chief Woman by the Shoshone and Water White Woman (or Person) by Rees, not knowing that Paraivo was a Comanche title and name.

[21] Hebard, *Sacajawea*, p. 93.

[22] Tinling, *Sacajawea's Son*, p. 27

[23] Howard, *Sacajawea*, p. 162. There is an intriguing record of the baptism of a daughter, Victoire, of Joseph Vertifeulle and Elizabeth Carboneau on April 23, 1843, in Westport, MO. It is possible that the mother was the Lizette born to Sacajawea and Toussaint Charbonneau. But there were many Charbonneaus in the Missouri region; Stella Drumm lists another, unrelated Toussaint Charbonneau (Luttig, *Journal*, p. 139–140).

[24] Tinling, *Sacajawea's Son*, pp. 24–29.

[25] Howard, *Sacajawea*, p. 189.

[26] Hebard, *Sacajawea*. pp. 221, 222.

[27] *Ibid.*

[28] Tinling, *Sacajawea's Son*, p. 77. See also Hebard, *Sacajawea*, p. 140, 141. Hebard believed the reference to Tessou was to a half-brother of Baptiste, Toussaint, who was also at the fort at that time. Baptiste is referred to by name and extensively described by W. M. Boggs as the boy who accompanied his mother and father on the Lewis and Clark expedition. This is the only place where Hebard gives evidence of the adult existence of the presumed half-brother of Baptiste who supposedly was adopted by Captain Clark and raised by Sacajawea. "Tessou" may have been a half-brother by another wife of Charbonneau, not the presumed Otter Woman.

[29] John Roberts to the editor of *The Oregonian*, 6/28/1905. Hebard files, American Heritage Center, Laramie, WY.

[30] *Ibid.*

[31] C. G. Coutant, *The History of Wyoming*, vol. I (Laramie, WY, 1899), pp. 668–670.

[32] Hebard, 1932, *Sacajawea*, pp. 195–196.

[33] Howard, *Sacajawea*, p. 89.

[34] F. G. Burnett to Grace R. Hebard, October 21, 1923. Hebard files, AHC, Laramie, WY.

[35] Hebard, *Sacajawea*, p. 195.

[36] F. G. Burnett testimony to Grace Hebard, March 1921, MSS 299C, Wyoming State Archives. In Mackey, *Inventing History*, p. 68.

[37] Hebard, *Sacajawea*, p. 238.

[6]"f..

[38] Hebard, *Ibid.*, p. 235.
[39] Hebard, *Ibid.*, p. 239.
[40] Henry E. Stamm, IV, *People of the Wind River* (Norman: University of Oklahoma Press, 1999), p. 164.
[41] Patten to Hebard, May 31, 1905.
[42] Rees, *Madame.*
[43] Hebard to Commissioner Charles Burke, April 22, 1925. Hebard files, AHC, Laramie, WY.
[44] Hebard to Charles A. Eastman, February 13, 1925, Schroer Collection, AHC, Laramie, WY. In Mackey, *Inventing History*, p. 62.
[45] Ohiyesa (Charles Alexander Eastman), *The Soul of an Indian*, edited by Kent Nerburn. Novato, CA, New World Library 2001, p. 52. Originally published in 1911.

# 6
# Radio Waves Over the Grave

[1] Congressman Charles E. Winter to Charles H. Burke, Commissioner of Indian Affairs, August 20, 1923, National Archives.
[2] "Ten Songs" by Frederick Boothroyd, with lyrics by P. B. Coolidge. Coolidge Publishing Company, Lander, WY, 1925. Courtesy of Alfred and Audrey Ward, Fort Washakie, WY.
[3] Porter B. Coolidge to Grace Hebard, January 16, 1924. Hebard Files, AHC, Laramie, WY.
[4] Porter B. Coolidge to Grace Hebard, October 30, 1923. Hebard Files, AHC, Laramie, WY.
[5] Porter B. Coolidge to Grace Raymond Hebard, January 30, 1924. Hebard files, AHC, Laramie, WY.
[6] "Miss Large, Wyoming University Student, Descendant of Sacajawea, Indian Guide." Undated and unidentified newspaper clipping. Hebard files, AHC, Laramie, WY.
[7] Blanche Schroer, personal communication, 1997.
[8] "Descendants Meet." Esther and Bernice Burnette, great-great-granddaughters of Sacajawea, meet John Maxon, a great-great grandnephew of Meriwether Lewis. Newspaper clipping, no publication entry, no date given. Hebard files, AHC, Laramie, WY.
[9] Esther Burnett Horne and Sally McBeth, *Essie's Story: The Life and Legacy of a Shoshone Teacher*. Lincoln: University of Nebraska Press, 1998.
[10] Philip J. Deloria, *Playing Indian*. New Haven: Yale University Press, 1998.
[11] *The Problem of Indian Administration*. New York: Johnson Reprint Corp, 1971. Originally published by the Institute for Government Research, Lewis Meriam, technical director. Baltimore: The Johns Hopkins University Press, 1928. Known informally as "The Meriam Report."
[12] Paul B. Wilson, *Farming and Ranching on the Wind River Indian Reservation, Wyoming*, Ph.D. thesis, Department of Geography, University of Nebraska, 1972.

# 7
# A Big Mouth and a Pink Chevrolet

[1] Obituary of Blanche M. Schroer, *Wyoming State Journal*, July 8, 1998.
[2] Blanche Schroer, "Boat-Pusher or Bird Woman?" *Annals of Wyoming* 52, no. 1 (Spring 1980).
[3] Blanche Schroer, "Sacajawea: The Legend and the Truth," *In Wyoming* (Winter 1978): 21–43.

[4] Minnie Woodring, all articles are in *Wind River Journal:* "Sacajawea—Here at Wind River!," Nov. 3, 1978, p. 2.; "There's Proof Sacajawea Is Buried at Ft. Washakie," Nov. 24, 1978, p. 5; "Sacajawea's Story Is a Complicated One," Dec. 1, 1978, p. 2; "Pioneer Fin Burnett Swears He Knew Sacajawea," Dec. 9, 1978, p. 8; "Story Told to Bernice Twitchell by Hereford Family," Dec. 15, 1978, p. 9; "Bureau of Indian Affairs Investigation Burial Place of Bird Woman," Dec. 22, 1978, p. 3; "Sacajawea Buried at Ft. Washakie," Dec. 28, 1978, p. 4.

[5] Margaret Mead, discussion session, Annual Meeting, American Anthropological Association, Denver, 1966.

# 8
# The Clue in the Sun Dance

[1] Alfred Ward, personal communication, July 2006. Ward has an old postcard of a Sun Dance from around 1902. Bud and Esther LeClair told me the Sun Dance was brought back the year they were married—1923.

[2] D. B. Shimkin. *The Wind River Shoshone Sun Dance.* Bureau of American Ethnology Bulletin 151, Anthropological Papers No. 41. Smithsonian Institution Bureau of American Ethnology, 1953: pp. 397–484.

[3] Fred W. Voget. *The Shoshoni-Crow Sun Dance.* (Norman: University of Oklahoma, 1984), pp. 196–200.

# 9
# Paraivo, Chief Woman

[1] Daisy Ballard St. Clair, personal interview, July 2003.

[2] Thomas W. Kavanagh, personal communication, August 24, 2005.

[3] Patricia Alberts and Beatrice Medicine, *The Hidden Half: Studies of Plains Indian Women* (University Press of America, 1983).

[4] Ake Hultkrantz, "Yellow Hand, Chief and Medicine-man among the Eastern Shoshoni," *Verhandlungen des XXXVIII Internationalen Amerikanistenkongresses* (Stuttgart-Munchen: 12 bis 18, August 1968), Band II.

[5] Shimkin, *Wind River.* Governor Anza's report lists all the important people involved in the 1786 treaty between the Comanche and the Spanish, including "Oxamaguea," the son of the chief and interpreter or go-between. Shimkin believed that the Shoshone chief Ohamagwaya was unquestionably the same person listed by Anza (p. 413). A. B. Thomas in *Forgotten Frontiers* (Norman: University of Oklahoma Press, 1932, pp. 71–83) describes the treaty process, and Oxamaguea is mentioned as Ecueracapa's young son. The treaty held for a generation.

[6] *Ibid.*, p. 410.

[7] *Ibid.*, p. 409

[8] James Trosper, interview, July 2005. The *ninimbe* are little people, said to be about 6 inches high, who live in the mountains.

[9] *Ibid.*

[10] Shimkin, *Wind River*, pp. 411–413. Ohamagwaya may have been born about 1765. He is reported, along with his father, Chief Ecueracapa, as being at the signing of a treaty between the Comanche and the Spanish with Governor Anza in New Mexico in 1786.

[11] F. G. Burnett in G. Hebard, *Sacajawea*, p. 168.

[12] Granville Stuart, *Montana As It Is* (New York: Arno Press, 1973), p. 24. This book was originally published in 1865 and so is contemporary with both Paraivo and Pa:si. Bald Eagle is said to be *pass-ee-ah*. Patseese is undoubtedly the diminutive, "Little Bald Eagle."

[13] Hebard, *Sacajawea*, p. 207.

[14] All the Shoshone testimonies in Grace Hebard's *Sacajawea: Guide and Interpreter of Lewis and Clark* call the old woman Porivo (Hebard's spelling), with the exception of that of Edmo LeClair. All testimonies except Edmo LeClair's use the term "Porivo or Sacajawea." I believe that Grace Hebard inserted the "or Sacajawea" to give her readers the impression that Paraivo and Sacajawea were the same person. The proof is that Hebard used an incorrect spelling of the name Sacajawea that is a Shoshone-like version of the true name of the woman on the Lewis and Clark expedition, first found in the Biddle edition of the journals of the Lewis and Clark expedition, published in Philadelphia, 1814. That spelling was the one that came to be most common, Sacajawea. The Biddle edition is not used by scholars as it is riddled with errors and inaccuracies. The best authorities on this are none other than Lewis and Clark. Later scholars of both the Shoshone and Hidatsa languages have reaffirmed that the name is Hidatsa, means Bird Woman, and was pronounced Sa-ca-ga-we-ah with a hard g. Reverend John Roberts used the Biddle version's Sacajawea and mistranslated the name as Shoshone for Boat-Pusher. He was a well-intentioned man but not a professional, degreed linguist. Grace Hebard preserved a letter of Feb. 6, 1906, in her archives from the chief ethnologist of the Smithsonian Institution, W. H. Holmes. Holmes cited the linguist Washington Matthews' published Hidatsa vocabulary showing the Hidatsa derivation of the name.

[15] Paraivo is sometimes spelled Paraibo because *b* and *v* are allophones.

[16] E. A. Hoebel, *Memoirs of the American Anthropological Association*, 54, 1940, pp. 18–20.

[17] The title Paraivo is a well-documented Comanche word. Cf. E. A. Hoebel, "The Political Organization and Law-Ways of the Comanche Indians," *Ibid*, pp. 18–20. It means boss, leader, head (so-called peace chief). See also *Taa Numu Tekwapu?ha Tuboopu Our Comanche Dictionary* (Comanche language and Cultural Preservation Committee, Lawton, OK, 2003, p. 41). Here the meaning of "paraibo" is chief, peace chief, officer, agent, stepmother, leader, person in charge.

[18] Grace R. Hebard, *Sacajawea*, p. 317. Hebard indicates that Rees' original manuscript "Shoshone Contribution to the Lewis and Clark Expedition" was "in possession of the author" (that is, Hebard). None of Rees' materials were published in his lifetime.

[19] John E. Rees, "The Shoshone Contribution to Lewis and Clark." (*Idaho Yesterdays*, Summer 1958). Rees cites these additional names, and it is possible that Hebard obtained them from Rees as she had access to his papers (18 above). James Willard Schultz also makes liberal use of Rees' names and materials, including the idea that Charbonneau's other wife, Otter Girl or Woman did not accompany the expedition because she was pregnant. He makes her die in 1806. See Schultz, *Bird Woman: The Guide of Lewis and Clark* (Boston: Houghton-Mifflin, 1918). Hebard had no use for the idea that Otter Woman had died at the end of the expedition in 1806, since she needed to have her survive until 1812 to die at Fort Manuel Lisa in place of Sacajawea. Thus, it is not surprising that Hebard in the bibliography to her book on Sacajawea (1932) cites Schultz's 1918 book as "purely historical fiction" (p. 318). This article is edited from Rees' unpublished papers.

[20] John E. Rees, "Madame Charbonneau: The Indian Woman Who Accompanied the Lewis and Clark Expedition, 1804–06; How She Received Her Indian Name and What Became of Her." (Salmon, Idaho: The Lemhi County Historical Society, 1970). This is an undated letter by Rees to Commissioner of Indian Affairs Charles H. Burke, believed to be from the mid to late 1920s (David G. Ainsworth, ed.). It is possible that Rees' letter was prompted by Grace Hebard who needed an authority such as Rees to begin the investigation of where Sacajawea died, an investigation headed by Charles Eastman,

sent by Commissioner Burke. We know that Hebard advised Eastman and guided his investigation which concluded that the Wyoming theory was correct. Cf. Mackey, *Inventing History*, pp. 59–63.

# 10
## Graven in Stone

[1] Bud Boller, personal communication, July 2006. The Eastern Shoshone tribe commissioned Boller to design and execute the state of Sacajawea.

[2] G. Hebard to J. Roberts, 1/10/1936; J. Roberts to G. Hebard 2/20/1936. Hebard Collection, AHC, Laramie, WY.

[3] G. Hebard, "Address to the Shoshones of the Wind River Reservation," August 22, 1931.

[4] "Lewis & Clark Trek 125 Years Ago Echoed in Honor Paid Baby Carried by Sacajawea: Dr. Grace Raymond Hebard Commissions Stone Cutters to Prepare Two Granite Monuments," *Wyoming State Journal*, May 1933, p. 7. Hebard files, AHC, Laramie, WY.

[5] Author of the booklet *This Is the Sun Dance,* which I read to prepare myself for my first Sun Dance in 1966.

[6] "Dr. Grace Raymond Hebard Perpetuates Memory of Sacajawea in Two Monuments," *Wyoming State Journal*, May 31, 1933.

[7] *Ibid.*

[8] Photograph of Lynn St. Clair depicting Reverend John Roberts, Sacajawea pageant, 1935.

[9] "Symposium on Sacajawea," *Annals of Wyoming* 13, no. 4 (Oct. 1941): 161–194.

[10] "Historic Ceremonies Celebrate Unveiling Sacajawea Markier," *Tiger Rage* (student newspaper, University of Wyoming), October 2, 1941.

[11] "Monument to Sacajawea Is Dedicated by DAR," *Casper Tribune*, June 26, 1963.

[12] Irving Anderson, "Probing the Riddle of the Bird Woman," *Montana: The Magazine of Western History* 23 (Autumn 1973).

[13] Colby, *Sacajawea's Child*, p. 181.

[14] Heather Evagelatos, "Sacajawea Honored with Bronze: Sculpture of Shoshone Teen Erected at Sacajawea Cemetery in Ft. Washakie," *Lander Journal*, June 25, 2003, p. B-2.

# 11
## Honoring Sacajawea?

[1] Kenneth Thomasma, personal communication, July 2000.

[2] John W. W. Mann, *Sacajawea's People: The Lemhi Shoshones and the Salmon River Country* (Lincoln: University of Nebraska Press, 2004).

[3] Phyllis Worden, "Namaqua Daughters Donate Mural," *Namaqua Chapter NSDAR Newsletter*, Loveland, CO, Chapter, November 2006.

[4] Press release, "Reflections on Wind River Trip" by Mona Worley.

[5] Contemporary Lemhi Shoshone woman, personal communication, July 2006.

# Bibliography and Recommended Reading

Albers, Patricia and Beatrice Medicine. *The Hidden Half: Studies of Plains Indian Women*. Lanham, Maryland: University Press of America, 1983.

Anderson, Irving. "J.B. Charbonneau, Son of Sacajawea." *Oregon Historical Quarterly* 71, no. 3 (1970).

Anderson, Irving. "Fort Mandan: Its Historical Significance." *South Dakota History* 6, no. 2 (1976).

Anderson, Irving. "Probing the Riddle of the Bird Woman." *Montana The Magazine of Western History* 23, no. 4 (1973): 2–17.

Anderson, William Marshall. Dale L. Morgan and Eleanor Towles Harris, eds. *The Rocky Mountain Journals of William Marshall Anderson: The West in 1834*. San Marino, California: The Huntington Library, 1967.

Bataille, Gretchen, editor. *Native American Women A Biographical Dictionary*. New York: Garland Publishing, 1993.

Bradbury, John. *Travels in the Interior of America*. March of America Facsimile Series. Ann Arbor: University Microfilms, 1966.

Brackenridge, Henry M. *Journal of a Voyage up the Missouri, Performed in 1811*. In *Early Western Travels*, R.G. Thwaites, ed., pp. 9–166. Cleveland: The Arthur H. Clark Company, 1904.

Casagrande, Joseph B. "Comanche Linguistic Acculturation: I." *International Journal of American Linguistics* 20, no. 2 (1954–1955): 140–151.

Casagrande, Joseph B. "Comanche Linguistic Acculturation: II." *International Journal of American Linguistics* 20, no. 3 (1954–1955): 217–237.

Casagrande, Joseph B. "Comanche Linguistic Acculturation: III." *International Journal of American Linguistics* 20, no. 1 (1954–1955): 8–25.

Clark, Ella E. and Margot Edmonds. *Sacagawea of the Lewis and Clark Expedition*. Berkeley: University of California Press, 1979.

Clark, William, and Meriwether Lewis. In *The History of the Lewis and Clark Expedition*. Elliott Coues, ed. New York: Francis P. Harper, 1893.

Colby, Susan M. *Sacagawea's Child: The Life and Times of Jean-Baptiste Charbonneau.* Spokane: The Arthur H. Clark Company, 2005.

Comanche Language and Cultural Preservation Committee. *Our Comanche Dictionary.* Lawton, Oklahoma: Comanche Language and Cultural Preservation Committee, 2003.

Coolidge, P. B., and Frederick Boothroyd. *Ten Songs.* Lander, WY: Coolidge Publishing Company, 1925.

Coutant, C. G. *History of Wyoming*, Vol. I. Laramie, WY: 1899.

David, Robert Beebe. *Finn Burnett, Frontiersman.* Glendale, CA: The Arthur H. Clark Company, 1937.

Deloria, Philip J. *Playing Indian.* New Haven, CT: Yale University Press, 1998.

Farlow, Edward J. *Wind River Adventures: My Life in Frontier Wyoming.* Glendo, WY: High Plains Press, 1998.

Fremont, J. C. Report of the Exploring Expedition to the Rocky Mountains in the year 1842 and to Oregon and North California in the Years 1843, 1844. March of America Facsimile Series No. 79. Ann Arbor, MI: University Microfilms, 1966.

Fowler, Loretta and Regina Flannery. "Gros Ventre." In *Handbook of North American Indians*, Vol. 13, Part 2, Raymond J. DeMallie, ed., pp. 677–694. Washington, DC: Smithsonian Institution, 2001.

Hafen, Ann W. "Baptiste Charbonneau, Son of Bird Woman." In *The Mountain Men and The Fur Trade of the Far West*, Vol. I, LeRoy Hafen, ed., pp. 206–224. Glendale, CA: The Arthur H. Clark Company, 1965.

Hebard, Grace Raymond. "Pilot of First White Men to Cross the American Continent." *The Journal of American History* 1, no. 3 (1907): 467–484.

Hebard, Grace Raymond. *Sacajawea: Guide and Interpreter of Lewis and Clark.* Glendale, CA: The Arthur H. Clark Company, 1932.

Horne, Esther Burnett, and Sally McBeth. *Essie's Story: The Life and Legacy of a Shoshone Teacher.* Lincoln: University of Nebraska Press, 1998.

Hoebel, E. A. "The Political Organization and Law-Ways of the Comanche Indians." *Memoirs of the American Anthropological Association* 54, 1940.

Howard, Harold P. *Sacajawea.* Norman: University of Oklahoma Press, 1971.

Hultkrantz, Åke. "Mythology and Religious Concepts." In *Handbook of North American Indians Volume 11*, Warren L. D'Azevedo, ed., pp. 630–640. Washington, DC: Smithsonian Institution, 1986.

Hultkrantz, Åke. "Tribal Divisions within the Eastern Shoshone of Wyoming." *Proceedings of the International Congress of Americanists* XXII (1958): 148–54.

Hultkrantz, Åke. "Yellow Hand, Chief and Medicine Man among the Eastern Shoshoni." *Verhandlungen des XXXVIII. Internationalen Amerikanistenkongresses* II (1968): 293–304.

Hunsaker, Joyce Badgley. *Sacajawea Speaks: Beyond the Shining Mountains with Lewis and Clark.* Guilford, CT: The Globe Pequot Press, 2001.

Johnson, Thomas H. "Maud L. Clairmont: Artist, Entrepreneur and Cultural Mediator." In *Being and Becoming Indian: Biographical Studies of North American Frontiers*, James A. Clifton, ed., pp. 249–275. Chicago: Dorsey Press, 1989.

Jorgensen, Joseph G. *The Sun Dance Religion: Power for the Powerless.* Chicago: University of Chicago Press, 1972.

Jorgensen, Joseph G. "Ghost Dance, Bear Dance, Sun Dance." In *Handbook of North American Indians*, Vol. 11, Warren D'Azevedo, ed., pp. 660–672. Washington, DC: Smithsonian Institution, 1986.

Kavanagh, Thomas W. "Comanche." In *Handbook of North American Indians*, Vol. 13, Part 2, Raymond J. DeMallie, ed., pp. 886–906. Washington, DC: Smithsonian Institution, 2001.

Kavanagh, Thomas W. *Comanche Political History: An Ethnohistorical Perspective 1706–1875.* Lincoln: University of Nebraska Press, 1996.

Kessler, Donna J. *The Making of Sacajawea: A Euro-American Legend.* Tuscaloosa: The University of Alabama Press, 1996.

Luttig, John C., and Stella M. Drumm, eds. *Journal of a Fur-Trading Expedition on the Upper Missouri, 1812–1813.* St. Louis: Missouri Historical Society, 1920.

Mackey, Mike. Inventing History in the American West: The Romance and Myths of Grace Raymond Hebard. Powell, WY: Western History Publications, 2005.

Mann, John W. Sacajawea's People: The Lemhi Shoshones and the Salmon River Country. Lincoln: University of Nebraska Press, 2004.

Markley, Elinor R., and Beatrice Crofts. *Walk Softly, This Is God's Country: Sixty-six Years on the Wind River Reservation.* Lander, WY: Mortimore Publishing, 1997.

Meriam, Lewis. *The Problem of Indian Administration.* Baltimore: The Johns Hopkins University Press, 1928.

Miller, Wick R. "Numic Languages." In *Handbook of North American Indians,* Vol. 11, pp. 98–112. Washington, DC: Smithsonian Institution, 1986.

Morgan, Dale L. "Washakie and the Shoshoni, Parts I, II, III, IV." *Annals of Wyoming* 25 (1953): 140–89; 26 (1954): 65–80; 27 (1955): 61–81, 198–220; 28 (1956): 80–93, 193–207; 29 (1957): 86–102, 195–227; 30 (1958): 53–89.

Moulton, Gary E., ed. *The Journals of the Lewis and Clark Expedition*, Vols. 3, 4, 9, 10. Lincoln: University of Nebraska Press, 1987–1995.

Nelson, W. Dale. Interpreters with Lewis and Clark: The Story of Sacajawea and Toussaint Charbonneau. Denton: University of North Texas Press, 2003.

Oglesby, Richard Edward. *Manuel Lisa and the Opening of the Missouri Fur Trade.* Norman: University of Oklahoma Press, 1963.

Ohiyesa (Charles A. Eastman). *The Soul of an Indian and Other Writings from Ohiyesa.* Kent Nerburn, ed. Novato, CA: New World Library, 2001.

Pence, Mary Lou. "Ellen Hereford Washakie of the Shoshones." *Annals of Wyoming* 22, no. 2 (1950): 2–11.

Peregoy, Robert M. "Nebraska's Landmark Repatriation Law: A Study of Cross-Cultural Conflict and Resolution." In *Contemporary Native American Political Issues*, Troy R. Johnson, ed. Walnut Creek, CA: Alta Mira Press, 1999.

Prucha, Francis Paul. American Indian Policy in Crisis: Christian Reformers and the Indian 1865–1900. Norman: University of Oklahoma Press, 1976.

Rees, John E. *Idaho Chronology, Nomenclature, Bibliography.* Chicago: W. B. Conkey Company, 1918.

Rees, John E. "The Shoshoni Contribution to Lewis and Clark." *Idaho Yesterdays* (Summer 1958): 2–13.

Rees, John E. *Madame Charbonneau; the Woman Who Accompanied the Lewis and Clark Expedition.* Salmon, ID: The Lemhi County Historical Society, 1970.

Reports to the Commissioner of Indian Affairs: Shoshoni Agency, Wyoming: (1873): 429, 612–613; (1874); (1876): 556–557; (1878): 651; (1878); (1879); (1883): 371–372, 778, 952; (1884); (1887): 313–315; (1890): 242–245. Washington, DC.

Ronda, James P., ed. *Voyages of Discovery: Essays on the Lewis and Clark Expedition.* Helena: Montana Historical Society Press, 1998.

Ronda, James P. *Lewis and Clark among the Indians.* Lincoln: University of Nebraska Press, 1984.

Ross, Alexander, and Kenneth A. Spaulding, eds. *The Fur Hunters of the Far West.* Norman: University of Oklahoma Press, 1956.

Russell, Osborne. *Journal of a Trapper.* Lincoln: University of Nebraska Press, 1965. (Originally published in 1955 by the Oregon Historical Society.)

Scherer, Joanna Cohan. *A Danish Photographer of Idaho Indians: Benedicte Wrensted.* Norman: University of Oklahoma Press, 2006.

Schroer, Blanche. "Boat-Pusher or Bird Woman? Sacagawea or Sacajawea?" *Annals of Wyoming* 52, no. 1 (Spring 1980): 46–54.

Schroer, Blanche. "Sacajawea: The Legend and the Truth." In *Wyoming* (Winter 1978): 21–43.

Schultz, James Willard. *Bird Woman: Sacagawea's Own Story.* Boston: Houghton Mifflin Company, 1918.

Shaul, David. "The Meaning of the Name Sacajawea." *Annals of Wyoming* 44 (Fall 1972): 237–240.

Shimkin, D. B. "Shoshone-Comanche Origins and Migrations," pp. 17–25 in Vol. 4 of Proceedings of the 6th Pacific Science Congress of the Pacific Science Association. July 24–August 12, 1939. 5 vols. Berkeley: University of California Press.

Shimkin, D. B. "Dynamics of Recent Wind River Shoshone History." *American Anthropologist* 44, no. 3: 451–462.

Shimkin, D. B. "Eastern Shoshone." In *Handbook of North American Indians*, Vol. 11, Warren L. D'Azevedo, ed., pp. 308–335. Washington, DC: Smithsonian Institution, 1986.

Shimkin, D. B. "Introduction of the Horse." In *Handbook of North American Indians*, Vol. 11, Warren L. D'Azevedo, ed., pp. 517–524. Washington, DC: Smithsonian Institution, 1986.

Shimkin, D. B. *The Wind River Shoshone Sun Dance.* Smithsonian Institution Bureau of American Ethnology Bulletin 151, Anthropological Papers No. 41. Washington, DC: United States Government Printing Office, 1953.

Stamm, Henry E, IV. *People of the Wind River: The Eastern Shoshones 1825–1900.* Norman: University of Oklahoma Press, 1999.

Stewart, Frank Henderson. "Hidatsa." In *Handbook of North American Indians*, Vol. 13, Part 1, Raymond J. DeMallie, ed., pp. 329–348. Washington, DC: Smithsonian Institution, 2001.

Stuart, Granville. *Montana As It Is.* New York: C.S. Westcott, 1865.

Swagerty, William. "Marriage and Settlement Patterns of Rocky Mountain Trappers and Traders." *The Western Historical Quarterly* (April 1980): 159–180.

Thomas, A. B. *Forgotten Frontiers: A Study of the Spanish Indian Policy of Don Juan Bautista de Anza, Governor of New Mexico 1777–1787.* Norman: University of Oklahoma Press, 1932.

Thomasma, Kenneth. *The Truth about Sacajawea*. Jackson, WY: Grandview Publishing Company, 1997.

Thwaites, Rueben Gold, ed. *Original Journals of the Lewis and Clark Expedition, 1804–1806*, I–VII. New York: Antiquarian Press, 1959.

Tinling, Marion. *Sacagawea's Son: The Life of Jean-Baptiste Charbonneau*. Missoula, MT: Mountain Press Publishing Company, 2001.

Trenholm, Virginia Cole, and Maurine Carley. *The Shoshonis, Sentinels of the Rockies*. Norman: University of Oklahoma Press, 1964.

Voget, Fred W. "Individual Motivation in the Diffusion of the Wind River Shoshone Sun Dance to the Crow Indians." *American Anthropologist* 50 (1948): 634–646.

Voget, Fred W. *The Shoshoni-Crow Sun Dance*. Norman: University of Oklahoma Press, 1984.

Wenzel, Janell M. *Dr. Grace Raymond Hebard as Western Historian*. Master's thesis, University of Wyoming, 1960.

Wilson, Paul. "Farming and Ranching on the Wind River Indian Reservation, Wyoming." Ph.D. dissertation, University of Nebraska—Lincoln, 1972.

*Wind River Journal* (newspaper published in Lander, WY) Nov. 3, 1978; Nov. 24, 1978; Dec. 1, 1978; Dec. 9, 1978; Dec. 15, 1978; Dec. 22, 1978; Dec. 28, 1978.

# Web Sites

The Eastern Shoshone—www.easternshoshone.net

The Lemhi Shoshone—www.lemhi-shoshone.com

The Shoshone-Bannock—www.shoshonebannocktribes.com

# Student Study Guide

*Also Called Sacajawea: Chief Woman's Stolen Identity* is an intentional departure from traditional ethnography. It does not describe modern Eastern Shoshone culture in broad, general strokes. Instead, it shows how an ethnographer does research by asking questions, developing new problems out of those questions, and using a variety of sources and approaches to arrive at solutions. The study draws on history—but also shows how approaches coming out of one's own culture affected interpretations of both Euro-American and Shoshone history. Anthropology progresses as more knowledge and objectivity are gained. As a result, *Also Called Sacajawea* shows how the clash between a dominant and subordinate culture can result in a revision of the past.

## The Lewis and Clark Expedition

In-depth knowledge of the Shoshone woman who accompanied the Lewis and Clark expedition is not necessary for this book. The *National Geographic's* DVD "Lewis and Clark: Great Journey West" is an excellent, 70-minute overview. Resources about the expedition and its members can also be found at www.nps.gov/jeff/LewisClark2/CorpsofDiscovery/CorpsofDiscoveryMain.htm and www.pbs.org/lewisandclark.

## Critical Thinking

The following questions for critical thinking can be considered as you read the book or they can serve as kindling for exploring topics associated with this text:

1. Do you agree with the way the U.S. government treated the Indians in the early reservation period? If yes, describe the specific actions. If no, explain the actions and what the government could have done differently.

2. Think about historical facts that you learned in history classes, such as the Salem Witch trials, Custer's Last Stand, or the Iraq conflict. What different interpretations of these or other events in American history can you think of?

3. Was Hebard's Ph.D. valid? Did having a Ph.D. in Political Economy prove that she had the skills to conduct research and qualify her as a researcher of merit? What skills would a researcher need to accomplish the search for what happened to Sacagawea?

4. Did Prince Paul receive any benefits from bringing Jean-Baptiste to Germany and educating him there?

5. What role do the media play in publishing the truth? In publishing false information? How do we know if something we read in a magazine or a newspaper or online is true?

# 1
# Here Lies Sacajawea

The chapter introduces both the author and the Eastern Shoshone of Wyoming's Wind River reservation. In 1966, Tom Johnson made his first visit to Wind River. He was an anthropology graduate student, there to learn whatever the Shoshone wanted to teach him about their culture. His hosts drive him around the reservation, especially proud to point out Sacajawea's grave. She returned to Wind River as an old woman and died there, they said.

The blurring of past and present is an important theme of this book; the two are inseparable in both understanding contemporary Shoshone and untangling the story of the Wind River Sacajawea. This chapter briefly describes the pre-reservation past of the Eastern Shoshone and their present-day situation.

## Questions for Discussion

1. How does the work of an anthropologist differ from other kinds of jobs?

2. "It took me years to listen deeply enough," the author says. Why would it be important for an anthropologist to observe, record, and remember many details? Why is it so important to listen closely and record and remember many details in conversations?

3. Who lives on the Wind River reservation? Why do they live there?

## Topics for Research and Report Writing
- Northern Arapaho
- Hunting and Gathering Societies

# 2
# Mistaken Identity

Readers take a Jeep drive on today's Wind River Indian Reservation, home to both the Eastern Shoshone and Northern Arapaho tribes, with stops at a reservoir, a sign to Sacajawea's grave, the trading post, and the Sacajawea Cemetery where Sacajawea and the former papoose of the Lewis and Clark expedition are memorialized. Except that this branch of the Shoshone was not Sacajawea's. She was Agaidika (Salmon-Eater) Shoshone, now called the Lemhi Shoshone from northern Idaho. Nevertheless, the architect of the Wind River Sacajawea theory, Grace Hebard, believed strongly that Sacajawea had returned to Wind River even though she did not come from the Wyoming Shoshone bands. In 1955, William Clark's cashbook from the 1820s was discovered. On its back cover, Clark listed the names of the members of the expedition. After *Se-car-ja-weau*, he wrote *Dead*. By this time, however, the idea of the Wind River Sacajawea was firmly implanted on the reservation. Few knew or cared what was now known. It mattered only what people believed.

## Questions for Discussion

1. In the early 20th century, times were hard for the Wind River Shoshone. Explain why the white authority structure would encourage the idea that Sacajawea had "returned" to her people. Why do some, such as the Daughters of the American Revolution, continue to honor her at Wind River?

2. Who was Grace Hebard? How did she make sure the Wind River Sacajawea would live on in memory?

## Topics for Research and Report Writing

- Euro-American Funerary Customs vs. Shoshone Funerary Customs
- Indian Agents
- Tourism and Its Effect on Indians

# 3
# How One Family Became Another

Tom is told that a recently deceased woman's family was descended from Sacajawea and that the family's name was originally *Charbonneau*, as in Toussaint Charbonneau, the name of the French-Canadian who took Sacajawea as his concubine. The name *Charbonneau* bothers Tom because no one on the reservation today carries that name and it does not appear in any census of the Eastern Shoshone from the early days of the reservation. There is no mention of Sacajawea at Wind River in the early reports to the Commissioner of Indian Affairs in Washington, D.C.

Recent scholarship shows that Sacajawea's son, Jean-Baptiste Charbonneau, died and was buried in Danner, Oregon, in 1866. Information about the man buried in Danner conforms to what we know about Jean-Baptiste Charbonneau—he was well-educated and spoke several European languages well. The man identified as Jean-Baptiste at Wind River does not match in any way the historical Jean-Baptiste Charbonneau. If Jean-Baptiste Charbonneau is not buried at Wind River, could there be a mistake about Sacajawea, too?

## Questions for Discussion

1. Describe the differences between the Jean-Baptiste Charbonneau who died in Oregon and the one who died at Wind River. Could they have been the same man?

2. Who were the *a-va-je-mear*? How did they get confused with Lewis and Clark?

3. None of the reports of the Wind River reservation superintendents before 1907 mention Sacajawea. Why is this a cut-off date? What are some of the reasons it is not plausible that Sacajawea's identity was being kept secret by the Shoshone?

4. What are some of the things Tom thinks would have been documented if the woman with the Lewis and Clark expedition had really lived at Wind River? Do you agree with him?

## Topics for Research and Report Writing

• Sweat Rituals
• Mountain Men Trading Rendezvous
• Chief Washakie

# 4
# Reservation and Town

The subject is money, from well-heeled outsiders gentrifying the neighboring town of Lander to partial victory in court for the Shoshone. Indians aren't as welcome in Lander as they once were. Non-Indians are welcome at the tourist spots on the reservation. Otherwise, the Shoshone don't want the reservation overrun with tourists.

The permanent Northern Arapaho presence at Wind River is now accepted by the Shoshone. The trail of broken promises and treachery goes back to the Brunot Treaty of 1872, which took South Pass with its gold mines and the Lander Valley. In 1904, the McLaughlin agreement ceded two-thirds of the reservation. Disease, poverty, and religious suppression took their toll. The Wind River Sacajawea theory couldn't have arrived at a better time.

## Questions for Discussion

1. What is the connection between the Sacajawea float and the granddaughter of Reverend John Roberts in the two Fourth of July parades?

2. Why do some Shoshone participate in the One Shot Antelope Hunt yet others block off the only road to a popular camping area and trailhead?

3. Tom believes that after the compensation of more than four million dollars, "the Shoshone had gained a partial victory but a very costly one." What does he mean? Do you agree with him?

4. Give examples of Indian visibility in Lander now and in the past. Why has it changed? How do you think Lander could be more welcoming to Indians?

5. Conditions at Wind River prepared the way for the success of the Wind River Sacajawea story. Explain.

## Topics for Research and Report Writing

- Tunison Judgment
- Brunot Treaty (1872)
- McLaughlin Agreement (1904)
- Ghost Dance
- Effects of Diseases on Native American Populations

# 5
# The Search for Proof You Can See and Touch

Professional historians have challenged Hebard's theory since the 1920 publication of the journal of the clerk at Manuel Lisa's fort. In his entry for December 20, 1812, John Luttig wrote that "the Wife of Charbonneau a Snake Squaw" had died. Although he doesn't name her, that woman had to be the one who accompanied Lewis and Clark's expedition.

This chapter explains how Grace Hebard lied and twisted the evidence in a desperate attempt to explain away John Luttig's journal entry and other contemporaneous documents. About this time, a third white man at Wind River, the former "boss" farmer, was enlisted to bring his garbled recollections of Sacajawea from the 1870s into the story. So desperate was Hebard to find props to her story that she decided that physical evidence was needed to settle whether or not Sacajawea had "come back" to Wind River. The Bureau of Indian Affairs sent a Sioux homeopathic physician, Ohiyesa/Dr. Charles Eastman. Eastman allowed Hebard to coach him about the facts surrounding Sacajawea. Unsurprisingly, he found that Sacajawea had indeed "returned" to Wind River and had died there, despite Eastman's unsuccessful search for physical evidence. Now Grace Hebard could claim that the United States government endorsed her theory and research.

## Questions for Discussion

1. What is the evidence that "the Wife of Charbonneau a Snake Squaw" who "died of a putrid fever" at Fort Manuel Lisa on December 20, 1812, was the woman who accompanied the Lewis and Clark expedition?

2. Who did Grace Hebard accuse of lying? Was she justified in making the accusation(s)?

3. Who was Otter Woman? Why was she necessary to Grace Hebard's theory of the Wind River Sacajawea?

4. Six-year-old Jean-Baptiste remained in St. Louis in the care of Captain Clark, who had promised to educate him, while his parents traveled up the Missouri to the Mandan villages. What are your views about this?

5. The Wind River Sacajawea theory rests largely on the recollections of Reverend John Roberts, James Patten, and Finn Burnett. Are their recollections reliable? Why or why not?

6. The title of this chapter, "The Search for Proof You Can See and Touch," refers to proof that goes beyond documents and recollections. At what point did tangible proof of the Wind River Sacajawea become desirable? Was it found?

7. Who is said to have sometimes worn a Jefferson medal? Who looked for the medal and why? Who was present at Bazil's exhumation? Who probably wasn't? If the medal had been found, would it have proved that Sacajawea had lived and died at Wind River?

8. Two other pieces of physical proof were said to exist. What were they? If either had been found, would it have proved that Sacajawea had lived and died at Wind River?

## Topics for Research and Report Writing

- Acceptance of Northern Arapaho by Eastern Shoshone
- The Mandan and Ethnic History
- Educating Native Americans in Europe
- Teaching Indians How to Farm

# 6
# Radio Waves over the Grave

The stereotypes of the Indian Princess (Sacajawea), the Faithful Sidekick (previous portrayal of Indians on the radio), and the Nature's Child (Boy Scout lore) obscure the truth of life at Wind River, which is often harsh. Per capita payments are a pittance, and land allotments have been divided and divided again as they are passed down and so are too small to till profitably.

## Questions for Discussion

1. List the Sacajawea memorials and commemorations at Wind River and in Lander, real and never-realized, mentioned in this book. To your knowledge, which were proposed, overseen, or paid for by Shoshone? Is memorializing the dead a traditional Shoshone value?

2. By the 1920s, the Wind River theory was in trouble. Why? How did Grace Hebard respond?

3. Hopi Anthropologist Wendy Rose has said, "Somebody is benefiting by having Americans ignorant [about] what European Americans have done

to them." Who benefits from stereotypes of Indians, such as those mentioned in this chapter?

## Topics for Research and Report Writing

- Perspective that Indians Are Nature's Children
- Presence and Types of Statues in a Town or City Commemorating Indians
- Indian High Schools and Colleges

# 7
# A Big Mouth and a Pink Chevrolet

An argument between Blanche Schroer of Lander and Maud Clairmont of Wind River reveals the emotional side of family history. Maud staunchly defends her grandfather's recollections of Sacajawea. Shoshone history is based on oral, not written, traditions. Blanche, however, is convinced that Grace Hebard used the recollections to create the Wind River Sacajawea myth and to deceive the Shoshone. Many, both Shoshone and white, remain convinced that Sacajawea lived to an advanced age and died at Wind River.

## Questions for Discussion

1. Family history often involves elaboration of the exploits of ancestors, or who they were related to. How can we interpret Margaret Mead's remark, "We all have ancestors who had castles in Wales?"
2. Why would so many Shoshone want to believe they were descended from Sacajawea?
3. Why do you think many in our culture make a hobby out of finding out more about deceased relatives?

## Topics for Research and Report Writing

Look at your own family history. See if you can discover a story, person, or event that influenced or changed your family in some way. Describe it, and discuss what could make it true or false.

# 8
# The Clue in the Sun Dance

It is 1966 and Tom takes part in a Shoshone Sun Dance put up to end the Vietnam War and to pray for the men in combat. He learns not only the sequence of the three-day ceremony but also its deeper, personal meaning. The next summer, Tom dances in another Shoshone Sun Dance put up by a different Sun

Dance chief for different reasons. Many years later, Tom realizes that the Sun Dance holds the major clue to the true identity of the Wind River Sacajawea.

## Questions for Discussion

1. The Sun Dance is not a ceremony where everybody is welcome. Why did Tom want to participate in the Sun Dance, and how did he obtain permission to go into it? What were the conditions that he had to accept?

2. What kind of interpretation of the Sun Dance did Lynn St. Clair provide, and how did his efforts create closer communication between whites and Shoshones?

3. Being a Sun Dance chief involves having a vision, but religious chieftainship may also be inherited. How did Johnny Trehero use ancestry to reinforce his leadership?

## Topics for Research and Report Writing

- The Transfer of Sacred Power in Shoshone Culture
- The Importance of Dreams as a Basis for Religious Inspiration
- What Kind of Power Does the Sun Dance Show?

# 9
# Paraivo, Chief Woman

In 2003, a visit to the Fort Hall reservation in Idaho causes Tom to investigate the traditional spiritual power of women in the Shoshone Sun Dance. The Sun Dance is an old tradition, one that goes far back in Shoshone–Comanche history. The great Ohamagwaya and his wife Paraivo brought the Sun Dance to the Shoshone from the Comanche. A series of deductions based on fieldwork led Tom to conclude that the woman now called Sacajawea at Wind River really was an important leader named Paraivo or Chief Woman.

## Questions for Discussion

1. How did Daisy St. Clair provide information that confirmed Tom's intuition that women played important religious roles in traditional Shoshone culture?

2. How did Tom usually obtain information from Shoshone people?

3. How did a visit to the Bannock Creek Sun Dance and stories of a Comanche prophetess contribute to an understanding of how not only Ohamagwaya, but also his wife, Paraivo, came to bring the Sun Dance to the Shoshone?

4. What other abilities and oral traditions contribute to our understanding of who Paraivo was and why she was important to the Shoshone?

5. How and why was Paraivo's true identity transformed into the American heroine, Sacajawea? Was the transformation accidental or deliberate? Why or why not?

## Topics for Research and Report Writing

- How Fieldwork Is Conducted
- Ethical Practices for Establishing a Relationship with Informants

# 10
# Graven in Stone

The statue of Sacajawea in the Sacajawea Cemetery symbolizes the Wind River Sacajawea's transfer of power and experience to Chief Washakie. The Wind River Sacajawea started with the historical Paraivo, and added to her identity that of the historical Sacagawea.

## Questions for Discussion

1. Give two examples from the chapter of how the Wind River Sacajawea is symbolically tied to Chief Washakie. What do those ties accomplish?

2. The Daughters of the American Revolution have memorialized the last resting place of Jean-Baptiste Charbonneau at both Danner, Oregon, and Wind River. Obviously, one body can't be in two places at once. Should both monuments be left standing?

3. The historical Sacagawea is not buried at Wind River. What monuments and other mementos would need to be corrected? Should they be left as is?

## Topics for Research and Report Writing

Access the Web site: http://www.sacajaweacenter.org. Assess the extent to which the information on the site coincides with Grace Hebard's Wind River Sacajawea. Is there any other example from history of how one person's identity was changed into another?

# 11
# Honoring Sacajawea?

From the 1993 Sacagawea U.S. postage stamp to the U.S. Sacagawea dollar coin to the Lemhi Sacajawea Center in Salmon, Idaho, to a Hunkpapa Sioux ceremony to honor the historical Sacagawea, the Wind River Sacajawea is more and more marginalized.

## Questions for Discussion

1. Grace Hebard, the three men who vouched for the authenticity of the Wind River Sacajawea (Reverend John Roberts, James Patten, and Fincelius Burnett), and local boosters told the Eastern Shoshone that Paraivo

had been the woman with the Lewis and Clark expedition. The Daughters of the American Revolution continue to tell them. Would you consider this a form of acculturation? Should the University of Wyoming (Grace Hebard's institution), the Episcopal Church (Reverend Roberts' institution), the Wyoming state legislature, and/or the Daughters of the American Revolution apologize?

2. Are the Eastern Shoshone partners in the makeover of Paraivo into the Wind River Sacajawea?

3. Voltaire said, "History consists of a series of accumulated imaginative inventions." How have the accumulated imaginative inventions of Grace Hebard and others affected today's Shoshone? Is this book respectful or disrespectful of the Eastern Shoshone?

4. Tom says, "Paraivo's spirit deserves honor, too." In your opinion, what are appropriate ways to honor Paraivo?

## Topics for Research and Report Writing

• The Hunkpapa Sioux
• The Lemhi Shoshone
• Fort Manuel Lisa—Then and Now